Jacques Vink - Piet Vollaard - Niels de Zwarte

BUILDING URBAN NATURE

TOWARDS NATURE-INCLUSIVE ARCHITECTURE

nai010 publishers

You are eager, and bold, and that's fine!
But prudence is the better part of boldness.
HEINRICH HEINE

Building Urban Nature, the Problem of Pioneering

Right after our previous publication *Stadsnatuur Maken / Making Urban Nature* came out in 2017, many of our fellow architects asked us: 'Nice and inspirational, this book of yours, but it says so little about buildings and architecture. What can I do as an architect?' This criticism was partly justified. Architecture was addressed, but merely as part of a set of urban typologies. *Making Urban Nature* was primarily focused on public space, ecological infrastructure and possible ecological measures at different urban scales. Moreover, as authors, we were also pioneering, as there was hardly any information available on the subject at that time. In a way, the publication was the first of its kind, certainly in the Dutch language and certainly given the connection it made between (urban) ecological insights on the one hand and urban and public space design on the other. But it barely discussed buildings and architecture. At the time, this was hardly possible because there were few if any built examples from that time, and nature-inclusive building had yet to take off.

With *Building Urban Nature*, we try to make up for this lack of nature-inclusive buildings and architecture. This time, we focus exclusively on the building and its immediate environment and the specific problems and challenges associated with construction and architecture. In this sense, it is a broadening of *Making Urban Nature* on a specific urban subfield: the building. As it concerns buildings, the recommendations and techniques are not only applicable in the city, but are equally useful for detached buildings in rural areas. As part of urban development, stone objects such as walls and quays are also included in this book.

Before we present information on flora and fauna on and around the building and on structural measures (especially regarding green roofs and facades), we briefly discuss the present state of affairs with regard to nature-inclusive building in a historical context. Then we indulge ourselves in some speculating about the near future, based on the current practice. The next chapter then deals with the need for nature-inclusive building and, in a second chapter, a vision of nature-inclusive architecture is discussed, including an inventory of nature-inclusive building types. We try to illustrate and substantiate the theory of the main text as much as possible through built practical examples. A number of sub-themes are also addressed in separate inserts. We conclude with the closing statement 'Ten Recommendations for Nature-inclusive Design' that will hopefully give the reader some food for thought and thereby help bring about a change in the building practice.

'Primitive Future Architecture', the House of Music in Budapest, (Sou Fujimoto, 2022).

As in the previous edition, we focus on the north-western European climate zone and have taken only realized projects as examples and as a source of inspiration. The latter is not easy, as there are not a lot of realized practical examples yet. Nature-inclusive building—like the urban planning practice of five years ago—is currently still very much in the pioneering phase. There is a lot of experimentation going on and, of course, sometimes things don't work out as planned. Many promises are made—and this is somewhat characteristic of designers (not just architects, nowadays also urban planners and landscape architects)—in renderings of exuberantly overgrown buildings surrounded by huge trees, fluttering butterflies and diligently nesting birds. We were extremely cautious in this sense and wanted to see things for ourselves first (we visited almost all the examples shown), preferably several seasons of flowering and nesting after completion. So the reader can actually visit every project discussed in this book. Initially, we set out in search of the realized ideal; buildings that pay attention to both flora (that was often the case) and fauna (a rarity), that fit in perfectly with the ecosystem of the immediate surroundings and that are at the same time of high architectural quality. Buildings that are thus truly designed and realized entirely nature-inclusively. We have found very few. For the time being, we mostly have to make do with projects that set an example in a specific area.

And then still, even if we solely publish realized projects and/or building sections, that does not necessarily mean that the nature-inclusive measures taken there also work in the longer term. Unfortunately, hardly any monitoring is done after completion, and when we asked the architects and ecologists involved whether the desired animal or plant species have established themselves permanently on the building or roof, we often got the answer: 'We don't know for sure. There is no monitoring, and there is no budget for it either.'
In general, this is a failing of the construction practice—after the building is completed, the architect takes some beautiful pictures and then withdraws. And even ecologists often do not return to the building they have been involved with for years. To date, dealing with change and the unexpected or unpredictable has been problematic as far as architecture is concerned (it is different for landscape and garden design; there, change over time is always a given). If this blind spot is ill-advised in general building practice, it is simply counterproductive in the pioneering phase of nature and ecology in and around buildings (which are, after all, subject to constant change) and ignores the essence of life: constant adaptation and evolution. Without feedback through monitoring, solid progress in nature-inclusive construction is not possible in our opinion: the only way to know the facts is to measure them.

With regard to information on flora and fauna, we confine ourselves in this publication to those species that are often found in or around buildings, who sometimes even depend on them and for whom meaningful supporting measures can be taken in or on buildings. These are often not the most spectacular (possibly threatened or protected) species, but they are those plants and animals that can (and often must) really be helped in the stony urban environment. In this respect, too, we try to avoid speculation and unsubstantiated promises. This is of no use to anyone and all too often leads to disappointment and ultimately to a negative assessment of the need for nature inclusiveness in general. And that will only lead us further astray.

Furthermore, the information offered is generic in nature, dealing mainly with general ecological and construction principles and common techniques. However, nature-inclusive building is always contextual and site-specific. For specific information about and opportunities and threats regarding local flora and fauna: consult an ecologist. For specific, local programmatic or structural options and challenges: consult an architect. Better still, let architect and ecologist work closely together and inspire each other from the very beginning of a design process. Only in this way will meaningful and perhaps innovative solutions come to fruition that advance the profession as a whole and preserve or boost the associated urban biodiversity.

Despite our misgivings about unproven, and therefore sometimes empty, promises, and despite the fact that for everything we present in terms of techniques and measures for species we use as much practical evidence and knowledge as possible, even we as authors have to add a caveat: we assume that everything we write about them is correct, but we are not always one hundred per cent sure. Simply because it is still too early to know for certain that the measures will work in the medium and long term, and also because too little research has been done on their longer-term effectiveness. And because there are sometimes multiple views within both the fields of architecture and ecology. This publication is therefore explicitly a running score in a longer process of advancing knowledge and possibilities of and for nature-inclusive design and construction.

That said, there is nevertheless much in the book that has been proven, that works and from which architects and the ecologists advising them can draw knowledge and inspiration. We hope this book inspires architects to make their practice nature-inclusive. Today, all too often the building and the built environment are still part of the problem. With Building Urban Nature, we want to kick-start building practices that are part of the solution and set the stage for a green, biodiverse and healthy city. Because it is necessary, but also because it is fun and inspiring.

Jacques Vink, Piet Vollaard, Niels de Zwarte
Rotterdam, September 2023

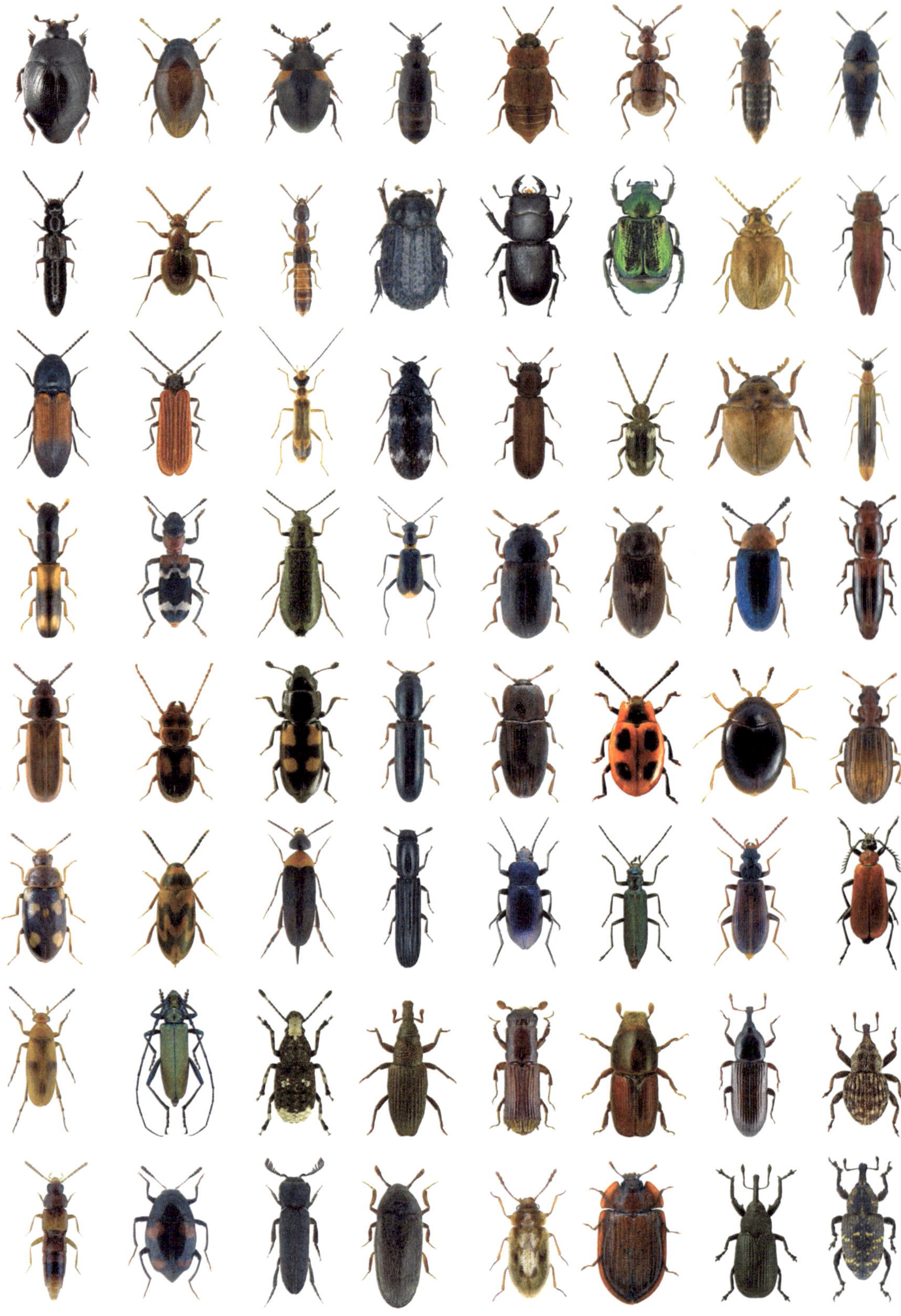

1

From learning about architecture, I found similarities in nature and a city. Both start small: in nature, a leaf; in a city, a bicycle, perhaps. There are large-scale similarities too: both have distinct eco-systems that thrive on their own qualities and resources.

SOU FUJIMOTO

Towards a Nature-inclusive Architecture

In this publication we describe the current state of affairs with regard to nature-inclusive building. The book presents what we can do today to invite nature to our buildings and give plants and animals a chance to live there. This leads to numerous questions. Will nature-inclusive design eventually lead to a fundamentally different architecture? And if so, at what scale level? Will new forms of buildings arise? Will it change the nature of the building's outer shell—the facade and the roof—in a fundamental way? Will inviting nature be limited to the outer shell, or will it eventually also reach the interior of buildings? Will it eventually lead to buildings that can constantly change in terms of composition and character, just like life itself?

At the moment, we can only speculate as to what the answers to these questions may be. As we said in the preface, we, the authors, have exercised great restraint when it comes to presenting speculations that have not yet been tested in practice, or—quite often false—promises. Nevertheless, or actually for that very reason, we feel the need to present a sketch of a possible future here and also speculate ourselves about a better world and a new (building) culture, especially about the architecture it may give birth to. And we are not alone in this. All sorts of nature attitudes, nature techniques and nature 'architectures' are popping up everywhere. In addition to the term 'nature-inclusive architecture' used by us, there is also ecological, symbiotic (in the Symbiocene), regenerative and 'life systems' architecture and experiments are done with 'living', biotic, biobased and bio-receptive techniques and materials. What all these 'new' architectures have in common is that we humans and/or architects will have to relate to nature in a different way and position ourselves *in* nature instead of beside it. This is also what we believe; without a fundamentally different attitude towards nature, we will get nowhere.

La cité des Étoiles, the terrace-shaped residential building in Givors, France, has in recent decades become overgrown like a natural rock formation, (Jean Renaudie, 1974/1981).

Von Humboldt and Bonpland describe the species they identify on Andean mountains and place them in their geographical context (depending on altitude and soil composition): the beginning of ecology. (*Geographie der Pflanzen in den Tropenländern*, Alexander von Humboldt and Aime Bonpland, ca. 1807)

The Long Road Towards a Common Ground

This may not be as hard as it may seem. After all, it wouldn't be the first time for humankind to fundamentally revise our attitude towards nature.

Prehistoric hunter-gatherers—and possibly also later nomadic peoples—obviously lived *in* nature and did not regard their own position in it as an exceptional, let alone a superior one. Nature was perhaps sometimes respectfully revered, but rarely feared or exploited. This relationship with nature changed when the first settlements were built and people began to practice agriculture and stock breeding. The result was a distinction between nature and culture. Livestock and crops, but also the people themselves, had to be protected against the wilderness; an outside world seen as hostile (wild, savage, and dangerous nature) became the opposite of a safe inner world of people and their domestic animals.

This separation was philosophically and culturally justified by influential thinkers such as Aristotle (around 350 BC), who placed humankind above plants and animals, which were void of reason. Later, monotheistic religions, especially Christianity, adopted this view of nature morality (humankind as ruler over creation).

The Chinese developed a quite different attitude towards nature. Taoism embraced nature in a much wider sense and already around the sixth century Taoist monks formulated the first rules for protecting nature. At the time, founder Lao Tzu wrote in the *Tao Te Ching*:

An image of man versus nature that has recently become iconic, and of the Romantic notion of the sublime. (*The Wanderer above the Sea of Fog,* Caspar David Friedrich, 1818) / Visitor parking space at Yosemite National Park; the sublime is still very much alive.

'The road (Tao) is Nature', and around 500 BC Confucius posited that 'nature and humans are integrated and inseparable'. This is in sharp contrast with views held by us in the West, where the Earth was considered as 'God-given' and therefore as something to be utilized. This led to an ever-increasing colonization and exploitation of nature.

Around the nineteenth century, when this exploitation reached its peak, a counter-movement developed and our attitude towards nature changed once again. First and foremost, by gaining more insight into the workings of nature, as biology—and especially the specialization ecology—began to study the natural world from a scientific perspective and understand and describe it as a coherent entity. One of the founders of this discipline was Alexander von Humboldt, who was the first to describe the interconnections between species and climate and soil of South America. That same period also gave rise to a different culture. During the Romantic era, poets and painters (who would later often become the first conservationists) began to sing the praises of the erstwhile savage, wild nature in positive and downright admiring terms. However, in many regards this attitude was still one of humankind versus nature. An important concept of Romanticism was the idea of the 'sublime': the awesomeness, danger and grandeur of nature was no longer feared, but rather admired. Caspar David Friedrich's painting *The Wanderer Above the Sea of Fog* (1818) is perhaps the most striking illustration of awe-inspired humankind confronted with sublime nature. This changing attitude to nature would eventually lead to establishing the first nature reserves. The world's first National Parks (in the USA: Yellowstone in 1872 and Yosemite and Sequoia, both in 1890) were clearly regarded as sublime nature. In the course of the twentieth century, the resulting nature conservancy has gradually led to increasing attention for nature values and ecological significance, apart from any sublime experience, and also to more attention for diversity and ecological coherence. From awe and admiration to empathy and protection, but even this protective attitude still positions humankind as 'keeper and steward' of nature opposite or at best next to nature, but not *in* it.

William Robinson's walled 'kitchen garden' at Gravetye Manor—which he worked on from 1885 to 1935—is part of a larger wild garden.

This late-nineteenth-century admiring attitude towards nature still prevails today, but once more a fundamental change is coming. One important moment in that change is the finding that we are by now living in a new geological era: the Anthropocene, the age in which the actions of humankind are visible everywhere on the planet and the consequences of those actions can be seen in climate change and the atmosphere. This notion stems from the so-called Earth System Sciences. The causes of these effects are basically known and can be summarized as human actions in the broadest sense. The consequences of these human actions on the Earth—and how big the negative effects are—are not really known yet but it is clear that the climate crisis and the partly related collapse of large ecosystems are a direct result.

Since the 1960s and '70s, various scientists, nature activists and philosophers have warned about the coming crisis and have also reflected on how we as humankind should respond to it. One of the first was James Lovelock who, together with Lynn Margulis, postulated the Gaia hypothesis, in 1974. In short, they proposed that living matter enters into an interaction with inorganic matter. In the process, a complex, self-regulating system evolves which in itself is capable of maintaining the conditions for life and keeping them in balance by means of negative feedback. Lovelock does give humankind a position in this, but not the most important one. Humankind is just another species and as such part of the much larger and more complex system. However, we now know that our influence on the system is much bigger than that of other species. French scientific sociologist and climate philosopher Bruno Latour states that we, humankind, in the period of modernization (roughly the period in which the Anthropocene slowly emerged) have moved ourselves to the space outside the planet and now look down from our 'spaceship' to the planet as if we were not part of it, as if we could very well live without

it. With this alleged non-influential position outside of nature we have given ourselves a licence to exploit the planet (just like Western religions did before). Of course this is a fiction: we cannot live without the planet, as we are intertwined with it and an integral part of it. In his book *Down to Earth. Politics in the New Climate Regime* (2018) Latour states that humankind has to (again) look for a common ground 'to land on' and for a roadmap towards a newly designed living environment that takes into account the new political, social and cultural regime. In that regime, in that place where we must land—here, back on Earth—the distinction between nature and culture is no longer tenable.
And so, after a number of changes, we find ourselves once again in a position where nature is—or for now let's say: should be—a 'natural' and integral part of our existence; a position in which it would be frankly life-threatening to go on wanting to set ourselves apart from nature.
In order to find a meaningful answer to the question 'what can architecture do?' architecture will first have to 'land' and go looking for a common ground where human-made things—including architecture—are inextricably intertwined with the natural world.

Options for a Nature-Architecture Fusion
In the English private garden tradition, the route towards the natural was embarked upon already much earlier. The influential book *The Wild Garden* (1870) by William Robinson is a to this day very modern-feeling—and practical—plea for applying native plants in more or less natural groups or families of plants in one's own garden. Subsequent maintenance should be limited to a minimum, according to Robinson: nature would find its own optimal order. So, 150 years ago—long before the species could literally not even be burned out of Western gardens and public parks—he warned against the danger of the rampantly proliferating, invasive Japanese knotweed. In Germany, in the first few decades of the twentieth century, Robinson's philosophy was adapted by garden architect Willy Lange into a more ecological approach and expanded towards the present-day plant sociology in a number of books under the theme of 'Nature Gardens'. In the Netherlands, more or less at the same time as Willy Lange, writer/teacher Jac. P. Thijsse promoted the attention for and application of native nature and plant sociology in the very popular Verkade albums and in his own magazine *De Levende Natuur* (Living Nature). He was also a founding figure of nature conservation and the so-called 'heemtuinen' (wildlife or habitat gardens). So, there has always been interest in a more ecological approach to garden culture during the twentieth century, albeit as a niche beside the more prevailing and definitely unnatural, modernistic garden and park culture.
Around 1970, the Frisian artist, 'wild-gardener' and self-declared 'ecotect' Louis le Roy revamped the wild garden tradition of Robinson and Lange and translated it into a 'nature-culture fusion', which culminated in the Eco-Cathedral in the Frisian village of Mildam, a project he worked on—in and with nature and time—from the 1970s until his death in 2012. The elements of process, the necessity of complexity, and involving residents in his projects were constants in his theory, which he expressed not only in a varied practice but also often in writing, especially in his book *natuur uitschakelen – natuur inschakelen* (disabling nature, enabling nature) (1973). Le Roy not only criticized the garden culture of neat flower beds and fake nature that was constantly tamed

On a field of several hectares, Le Roy initially let nature take its course, until he asked the municipality of Heerenveen around the 1980s to dump all remaining debris from repaving, such as paving stones, kerbstones et cetera, on his land from now on. Then for decades, using only his own 'free, and creative energy' and his bare hands, he built pile structures from it, which he released back to nature after 'completion'. This created a permanently changing interaction between culture (architecture) and nature. In his belief, future generations have to continue the work, with the provisional completion date being the year 3000. Eco-cathedral, Mildam (Louis G. le Roy, ongoing since ca. 1970, NL)

Waldspirale, Darmstadt. (Friedensreich Hundertwasser, Heinz M. Springmann, 1998-2000, D)

by 'maintenance' of his day and age, but especially also the architecture and urban planning, which he characterized as dead monocultures that were far removed from life and frustrated the deployment of the 'free, creative energy of city dwellers'. This book is also a plea for allowing nature to penetrate into the city along green corridors, a concept we now call 'Urban Ecological Network'. The Eco-Cathedral is not conceived as a functioning building to be used by people, but serves as a metaphor for the new, natural, and integrated architecture and urbanism of the future.

Nature-inclusive Future Architectures and Techniques

To return to the original question; 'what can architecture do and will the attention to nature lead to a completely new architecture?' the examples given here as yet represent no more than intermediary steps towards the ideal, because we deliberately chose to discuss only realized projects and techniques that have proven themselves in practice. Still, such intermediary steps are important and necessary; in a cultural development one cannot suddenly jump ahead and skip the necessary intermediary stages. In addition to the 'wild-garden movement', architects can first and foremost be inspired by the answers emerging around 1970 to the question of what architecture could or should do to restore the broken relationship between humans and nature. The best-known examples of this are the Ökologische Architektur of the German architect Ot Hoffmann of the Frenchman Jean Renaudie and the Austrian artist/architect Friedensreich Hundertwasser.

There are several ideas, techniques, nature-attitudes and -architectures that are not discussed because of our emphasis on realized projects. However, in this more speculative chapter they do warrant mentioning. In fact, we allow ourselves to present a small 'render' here, an 'artist impression' in words of our thoughts about developments towards a nature-inclusive architecture.

Biobased Materials and Techniques

Presently used building materials will change in the future. Biobased materials will increasingly replace building materials that are harmful to climate and the environment. There may still be a limited role for bricks and natural stone, but because of the high CO_2-footprint of its production process concrete is already a material of the past, despite the current experiments with so-called 'bio-receptive' concrete. Why not use bio-receptive, wooden prefab panels right away? Another advantage of prefab is that it can be produced more efficiently (both in terms of material and of energy) on a central location and—if cleverly designed—can be reused later (circular construction). If we manage to produce wood in production forests in a sustainable way, it will replace bricks, stone and concrete. The latter will probably remain the only possible material for foundations in the foreseeable future. The use of, for example, mycelium—fungi that can be shaped into building blocks—or of straw as an alternative for bricks are other examples of such biobased building materials. Depending on their footprint, synthetic materials will continue to be used but these too will increasingly be made from plant-based raw materials and no longer form fossil sources. Finally, the necessity of circularity (for both biological and technical cycles will more and more often become part of a regenerative building process. Also, the construction world will increasingly

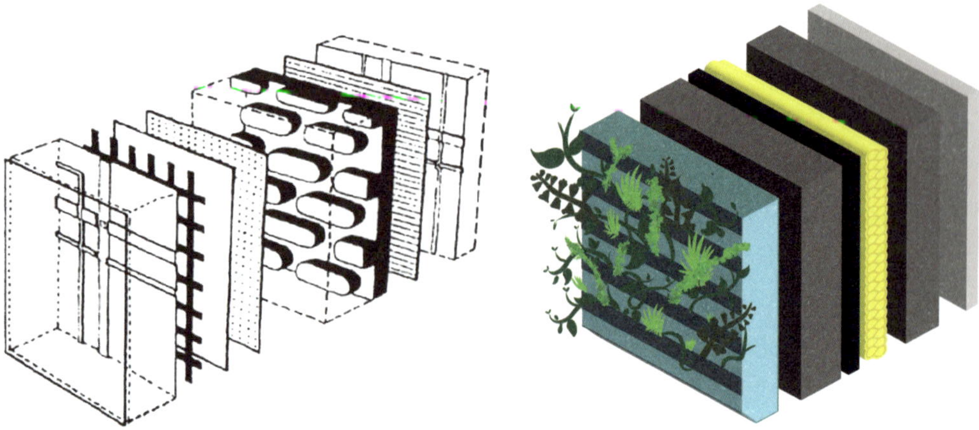

The 'Polyvalent Wall', a diagram by architect Mike Davies (1981), showing the various functional layers of a facade (system) / The facade is housing nature. This extra shell consists of two parts, the carrier and the growing. The biobased shell can also perform other functions, for example as a natural sun screen.

be paying attention to short cycles, in which both literally and figuratively as little distance as possible needs to be covered.

A Bio-based Outer Shell

We humans like to live and work in interiors we can control and where we can bring temperature, air humidity and air quality in line with the demands we put on those conditions at any given time. Modern architecture is thus characterized by a strict separation of the outside climate and the conditioned indoor climate. In 1985, British architect Mike Davies foresaw that the facade of the future would be an active one. Instead of passively protecting us against the elements, the facade would actively react to and mediate between wishes and actions from the indoor climate and the given outdoor climate. By now, his vision has become partly true and is applied to the modern-day facade package. However, this is still a far cry from comparing the facade to an intelligent computer interface.

From now on Davies' package of layers will have a new functional layer: the nature shell, in which plants and animals can live. This is not really a problem for the roof and there it is implemented already. With the facade however, for which Davies describes a number of different functions, things are trickier. Wall plants, for instance, are at odds with the function of providing a view and allowing daylight to enter. Birds and bats require some quiet around their breeding and living areas. Whereas on the roof a 'battle' mainly takes place between 'green' and 'yellow' (nature value and energy generation), with hardly any competition with human use, on the facade there is much more friction between humans and nature. Such conflicts can only be solved by 'reaching agreements' by integrating nature into the whole of functional and technological demands placed on the facade. Today this question is more urgent than ever, now that places to live for birds and bats are becoming scarce as a result of our modern building methods and the post-insulation of existing houses. Therefore, from both a legal and moral obligation, functional living areas will have to be created in the facades of the future in order to provide these species with a place to live.

According to architect Jean Renaudie (1925-1981), architecture should reflect the complexity and variability of life. Inspired by the shapes of nature and the earth, his vision resulted in overgrown stony landscapes such as La cité des Étoiles in Givors. (1974/1981, FR)

If this will indeed become fact, then the appearance of the facade, and architecture with it, will considerably change. Not only because the built main shape and therefore the facade too will be more porous, more varied and more uneven but also because closed surfaces that are in sight will no longer be made of concrete, wood or bricks, but will increasingly consist of living matter. This means that architects will to some extent have to let go of control over the appearance of the facade, as nature is dynamic and its predictability is limited. To us this seems to be only an advantage. It is a step towards a regenerative architecture that is more like life itself.
Then again, it's not that buildings will then be overgrown from top to toe, as many renderings of future 'green' architecture on the internet may suggest. In such proposals nature is dominant and has completely overrun culture (architecture). This is a caricature. The very point is that a meaningful fusion is created between nature and culture in which both experience as few negative effects as possible from each other; on the contrary: it should lead to mutual benefits, to a symbiosis.

Regenerative Architecture
Regenerative architecture looks for solutions in which things that grow also provide benefits to humans in the form of ecosystem services. Think of cooling, water management, and cleaner air. Biobased architecture can even have a constructional function: design studio Baubotanik uses living trees and plants as building material in hybrid constructions in which willows are not only part of the load bearing construction but also a habitat for insects, thereby providing food to birds.

Experiment with the constructive use of growing trees (Footbridge, Wald-Ruhestetten, Baubotanik, 2005, D)

Regeneration also has another meaning: time and again creating anew and adapting to a changing situation. This function is inherent in both life and nature, but not or not yet in buildings. 'A building is not something you finish. A building is something you start,' wrote Stewart Brand in his seminal book *How Buildings Learn* (1994). What he meant was that buildings should also be conceived as subject to permanent change over time. In thinking about how exactly this should occur much can be learned from biological and ecological principles. In any case, the present trend towards circular construction is a good start.

In 2011, environmental philosopher Glenn Albrecht postulated a new era, that of the Symbiocene, in which humankind, nature and technology forge a new balance. Putting aside the fact that you can't declare a new geological era every 25 years, he did point the way forwards. Ultimately (in a climax situation, in ecological terms) nature-inclusive architecture leads to a fully-fledged symbiosis between humans and nature. An architecture in which technique (built things) and nature (growing things) are inextricably connected; where technique cannot function without nature and nature cannot function without the technical foundation.

A Zoönome Architecture

'We envision a world where our extractive economy is transformed into a regenerative, human-inclusive, reciprocal Zoönomy: a network of exchange of matter, energy and meaning that supports all bodies in their existence. The Zoöp organization model contributes to ecological regeneration by including the interests of other-than-human life in organizational decision making.'

Urban Reef is a 3D-printed ceramic sculpture for nature to settle on. The project is equipped with sensors that monitor the microclimate inside the object. (Urban Reef, 2023, NL)

So reads the mission statement of the Zoönomic Institute, an initiative by the Dutch architecture and design museum The New Institute (2022). Among other things, it raises the question of whether and how we humans can give plants and animals a voice in political decision-making processes and what exactly the rights of animals are. From there one can also imagine a Zoönome architecture, a design and realization process in which animals and plants have an equal say in the decision-making. If this is applied consistently it will change architecture even though we cannot predict what this change will be exactly. Humankind would suddenly and radically be placed on equal footing with all other life—ecocentrism at its purest.

Initially, we, the authors, went looking for realized buildings that provided living space for both plants and animals, for this book. However, except for a rare exception, we didn't find any that also included accommodation for animals. Many architects—and perhaps their clients as well—appear to find it difficult to really grant animals access to buildings, in spite of the fact that there are a number of building-bound animals who—unlike plants—cannot live without our buildings. In an 'eco-just' building and decision-making process this would no longer be the case.

The Need for Monitoring

Nature-inclusive building is a pioneering practice in which some measures have demonstrable results were as other ones still need to prove themselves. By monitoring these measures for plants, birds, bats and insects we can learn what works and what doesn't. This can only be done through research and by gathering data. However, this takes a lot of time and money and requires consulting specialized ecologists. Also, monitoring is often just a balancing item in the budget, if it is included in the project

Knowledge about soil life and the interaction of that great diversity of life forms with trees and other plants, is still evolving.

plan at all. By linking sensors, smart cameras and other technical tools to projects, this research is expected to become less labour-intensive and more scalable in the future. We foresee a greater role for technology in this.
Monitoring also increasingly makes use of 'citizen science': people can make their own observations and upload them via internet (in the Netherlands via *waarneming.nl*, internationally via *observation.org*). They can also use the accompanying AI-app ObsIdentify, which is surprisingly good at identifying species from a photograph. In the Netherlands more than ten million observations are shared through this platform every year, including from urban areas. This is a treasure trove of information for science and provides more insight into the occurrence and distribution of species in space and over time. Using this new knowledge, architects can further improve their nature-inclusive designs.

The Need for Soil Research and Knowledge
Not only about plants and animals, but also about soils, there still is a lot to learn, More and more we are realizing that the soil with all its mostly hidden biodiversity is an essential condition for a healthy ecosystem. Within the framework of the new Dutch 'soil- and water-driven' policy, more attention is now given to the soil. For instance, in new building projects the ground is left untouched more often, preserving biodiversity and securing a better starting position for future aboveground communities. There have also been experiments with transplanting soil from the ground level to the roof; monitoring will show whether this is successful or not. Technology will also give a boost to our knowledge of the soil: by means of 'environmental' DNA testing (also referred to as e-DNA) it is possible to identify thousands of species of bacteria and fungi from a few grams of soil and learn more about the soil microbiome.

It is estimated that the soil contains no less than 59 per cent of all life forms, from microbes to mammals, making it the most bio-diverse environment on our planet. Charles Darwin described earthworms as 'nature's workers' and estimated that every so many years the complete surface layer of the world would pass the stomachs of earthworms.

Towards a New Design Practice

The topics described above unlock a new field of activity, the discipline of the 'ecological designer' or perhaps 'ecotect', moving between landscape design, architecture, and ecology. A discipline that requires ecological knowledge and design and monitoring skills. And above all courage: nature-inclusive architecture is a process, not a clearly defined endpoint.

The basis of nature-inclusive architecture is that we should change our attitude towards nature. By realizing that we are an inextricable part of nature. By being aware that nature will continue to develop and that we should design not against, but with nature. By looking for symbiosis, whereby architecture can help enhance urban nature. By making a brief on behalf of animals and plants and in doing so strive to give nature an equal voice in our decisions. And using this to work on the city and change our thinking from egocentric to eco-centric.

Idea sketch: Building Apart Together (BAT), (Studio Architectuur MAKEN, 2023, NL)

2

A building is not something you finish. A building is something you start.

STEWART BRAND

In 2020, the weight of human-made objects exceeded that of all biomass on earth for the first time. The rate of accumulation for anthropogenic mass has now reached 30 gigatons. As the rate of growth of human-made mass continues to accelerate, it could become triple the total amount of global living biomass by 2040. (source: Visual Capitalist, Bruno Venditti, Mark Belan)

The Need for Nature-inclusive Design

Biodiversity loss is occurring at an unprecedented rate. The causes are diverse and complex, but it is beyond doubt that human activities play a leading role in this. Industry, intensive agriculture and animal husbandry have a profound, negative impact on soil quality, ground and surface water, and biodiversity. Urbanization is also destroying natural habitats, and fragmenting the remaining food, shelter and nesting places.

In 2017, a research group published alarming statistics about the decline in insect populations at 63 sites spread across 31 German nature reserves. Counts conducted annually over a 27-year period showed a 76 per cent loss in the total biomass of flying insects. The news was a wake-up call for the world. It was not the first time that the loss of insects and other plant and animal species over the past decades had been demonstrated, but the magnitude in this short time frame and the fact that these were nature reserves came as a surprise even to ecologists.

In 2020, another study was published which stated that around that year, the total mass of human-made (anthropogenic) constructions became greater than the total biomass. Of course, that human-made mass is largely concentrated in our buildings. This includes metals, asphalt and stone. But most of it is concrete, a material that also has a major impact on climate change due to CO_2-emissions during production. Even within the biomass column itself, humans together with domesticated animals form a significant part. For example, more than 95 per cent of the biomass of mammals consists of humans and their livestock and pets. Intensive agriculture, developed to feed the growing populations in cities, resulted in deteriorating living conditions for plants and animals in the countryside. Hence, the decline in biodiversity is also attributable to increased urbanization. And if the problem is partly caused by the city, shouldn't we also look for solutions there? The anthropogenic mass, all human-made things including cities and their architecture, will have to be made in such a way that less, if any, harm is done to nature. This requires a completely different way of thinking and acting. So far, our buildings and cities have largely been thought of and made as 'non-natural'. They existed separately from nature and were even meant to protect against nature, against the weather, but also against animals deemed wild or harmful. Now that the impact of urbanization has become so profound, we can no longer afford this attitude.

For more than 50 years, scientists have studied and demonstrated the deteriorating state of climate and nature. A major milestone was 'The Limits to Growth', the Club of Rome report published in 1972. The report warned against the depletion of the planet's resources if the world's population continued to grow. In her 1962 book *Silent Spring*, Rachel Carson already warned against the overuse of pesticides, and predicted a spring when we would no longer hear birds singing.
These warnings led to a greater focus on nature and conservation in the 1970s, including in architecture and urban planning. So-called ecological gardening and ecological architecture were a trend for a while, but attention soon turned to limiting the use of the finite supply of fossil fuels and the search for sustainable alternatives. Nature seemed to be forgotten again for a while in the following decades.
However, later research showed that continued consumption of the fossil fuel supply would not only deplete it, but lead to a much more serious problem: rapid climate change due to increased CO_2-concentrations in the atmosphere. We now face the consequences of this climate change on a daily basis, and cause and effect are hardly denied anymore either. The world is slowly making the transition to reducing CO_2-emissions and using alternative energy sources.
But the climate crisis is not the only problem; it may not even be the most serious one. Simultaneously with global warming, we face several related problems that could collectively lead to the collapse of entire ecosystems.
The Stockholm Resilience Centre examines the dynamic interaction between human activity and nature, and published the chart 'Planetary Boundaries' with the thresholds that should not be crossed if humanity is to survive. The latest update of the 2023 diagram states that for every problem area, the boundary has now been crossed. To reverse or at least dampen its impacts, the world faces enormous challenges.

In itself, the natural system has proved extremely resilient from the very beginning of life. It has experienced several major extinction waves and survived massive changes in climatic conditions. But what is true of the system as a whole is not true of species individually. Large numbers of these disappeared in earlier epochs to make way for new species and new systems. The current crisis is therefore primarily a crisis of 'our' system, of the natural conditions, of the specific ecological cohesion that our human species to which our species is inextricably linked. So, 'nature' as a system does not need us and will adapt again after the next wave of extinction, with some surviving species and a larger number of new ones. But whether humans will still be part of it remains to be seen. It is our own species, *Homo sapiens*, that needs nature as it currently functions if we are to survive. Humankind is not separate from nature, but an integral part of it. If we want to preserve the system on which we depend for our survival, our human-made materials and human processes from now

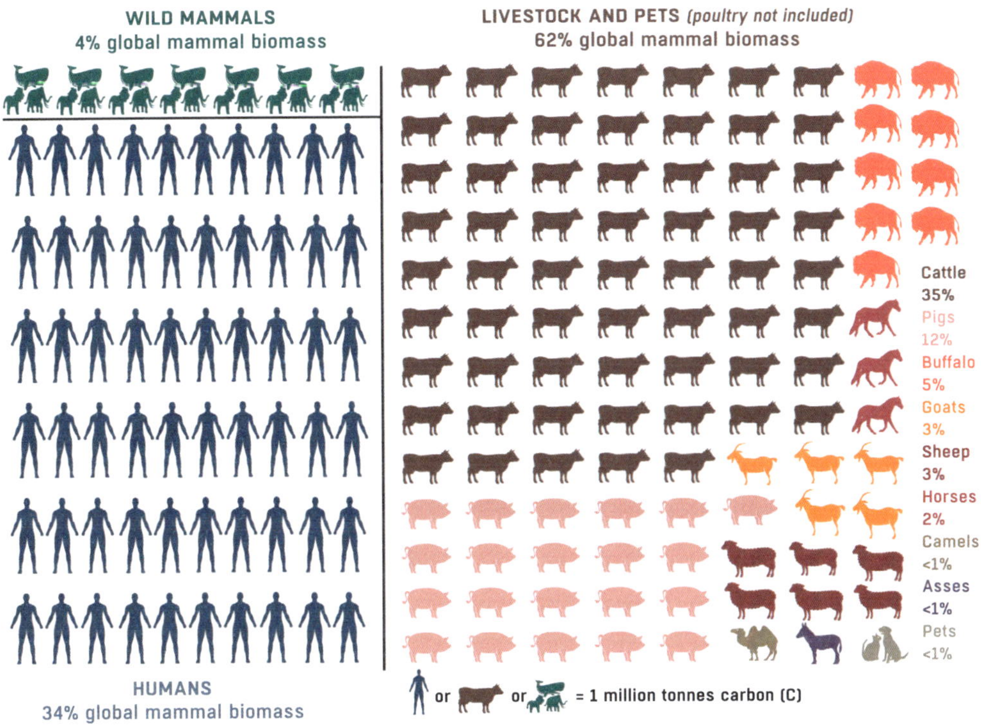

The total weight of mammals living in the wild pales when compared to that of us humans and our domesticated animals. (Source: Bar-On, Y. M., Phillips, R., & Milo, R. (2018). The biomass distribution on Earth. Proceedings of the National Academy of Sciences, 115(25), 6506-6511.)

on must be in the service of this system, or at least carried out in such a way that there is no further deterioration. Our cities and buildings then need to be developed as an integral part of the natural system, no longer nature-proof, but nature-inclusive.

Biodiversity and Resilience

Biological diversity, or biodiversity, refers to the variety of species, genes and habitats. This richness of life is closely linked at many levels both to all living organisms (biotic) and to the non-living environment (abiotic). Diversity is what makes life on earth possible: no single species would survive on its own. Instead, it is the whole, the entire web of species working together that sustains the complex system we call life or nature. The decline in species diversity therefore directly affects the 'health' of the system as a whole, and thus that of human beings in particular. The impoverishment of biodiversity and species decline can spill over into the whole (food) chain with consequences we cannot yet foresee.

The vulnerability of the system is highlighted, among other things, by the fact that almost all life on land takes place in an extremely thin layer between the treetops and the layer of soil life and circulating groundwater. Earth Science, the multidisciplinary science that studies the complex interaction of physical, biological and chemical processes on the planet, calls this thin layer of life 'the critical zone'. The resilience, the adaptability of life within this critical zone is defined as the degree to which this system is able to bounce back to its original state in the event

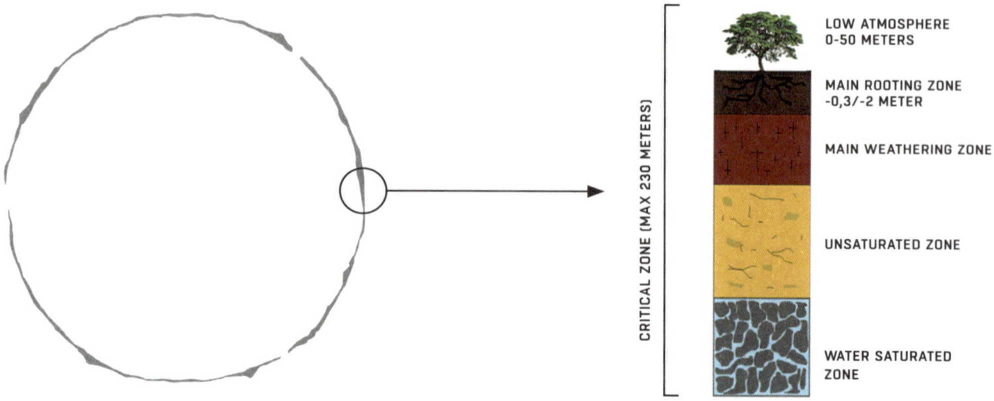

Critical zone: life essentially takes place in the earth's outer shell (down to a depth of around -220 metres) and in the lower 50 metres of the atmosphere.

of disturbances, be they natural or human-induced, or adapt in such a way that it evolves towards a new stable state.

In general, the resilience of a system is determined by a range of factors. Integrality is one such factor. An ecological system can be illustrated by the so-called food pyramid. It shows that different species are fully integrated and that all species are interdependent. In itself, this is a vulnerability. If an entire species group were to disappear, the cycle of energy and resources would be interrupted. In a resilient ecosystem, therefore, we see both complexity and excess (redundancy). In a food web, there are always multiple species with similar functions, and thus multiple pathways for the cycle to follow. If a species is lost due to disease or natural disaster, another species can take over a function. A certain distribution of species with their specific living conditions within a habitat is also important. If conditions change, for instance due to climate change, the system can 'move on' to a new stable state. The complexity of the system thus also determines its capacity to adapt. The history of the evolution of life is actually a series of adaptations and of increased complexity. Biodiversity is thus not only a characteristic of life; it is also a prerequisite for its survival.

It is about more than just genetic diversity; the sum of all the different species. Functional diversity, the role species play in the cycle and in specific ecosystems, is also important. Indeed, the resilience of the system is enhanced, among other things, by the presence of different species with similar functions. An even distribution of different species and their functions is another factor. An overabundance of a single species can lead to what we call a plague. This is sometimes part of the natural dynamic where feedback creates a new balance. For example: the mouse population is very high one year (a 'plague') which creates a high food supply for birds of prey and owls, which then increase in numbers, after which the mouse population decreases again in the following years, which in turn decreases the bird of prey and owl population and so on. On larger time scales, these are normal cycles in which species interact. However, such a process does not work when people introduce invasive exotic species. These species, intentionally or unintentionally transported, sometimes over long distances, can thrive too easily without their natural enemies and can disrupt,

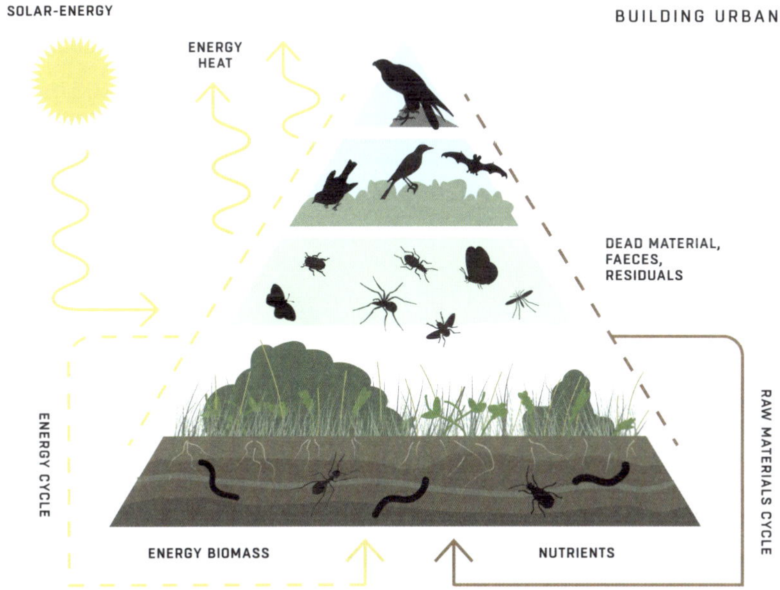

The food pyramid represents the closed loop of food (and energy) in the ecosystem. At the base are the reducers, the soil life that breaks down waste into nutrients. Above them are the producers, the plant world that captures carbon through photosynthesis, and the consumers, the animal world that eats plants and other animals. At the top of the pyramid are the predators, which eat other animals.

weaken and even endanger a system. The difference between an invasive exotic species and a 'regular' exotic species, is that the invasive exotic species is harmful and proliferating, and a 'regular' exotic species sometimes finds its way into a system and is simply a newcomer.

Whether it is a native species or an invasive exotic: the abundant presence of a single dominant species (think also of a monoculture) is rarely a good thing because it is unstable over time and too vulnerable. Such a system thus lacks resilience and other species are crowded out, simply reducing biodiversity. On the other hand, it is also not necessarily true that ecosystems with relatively few different species, such as a desert or an urban wasteland with pioneer vegetation, for example, would not be of value. On a larger scale, ecosystem diversity is also relevant. The relative richness and resilience of a system depend on various biotic (species and their functions and products) and abiotic ('non-living' conditions such as climate, soil and water conditions) factors. When abiotic factors change quickly, as in the city, or with rapid climate change, selection pressures can be high, making a species undergo adaptations in a short period of time. These are not always direct genetic adaptations, but are primarily behavioural changes in species that are not yet genetically recorded. Species may therefore behave differently in cities due to the influence of urban area dynamics from how they behave in quiet areas. Ecosystems also play a specific role in the planet's geo-chemical cycle. For example, the decline of tropical rainforests or algae in the oceans directly affects the balance of oxygen and carbon dioxide in the atmosphere.

Causes

The causes of biodiversity loss are diverse, but almost without exception related to human activity. The first is the extensive depletion of resources and land where

Asian knotweeds are a group of invasive exotic species, which disrupt the local ecosystem in Western Europe and can damage roads and buildings / The box tree moth is an invasive, non-native species that came from Asia via the buxus plants trade. The caterpillars strip bare the host plant in no time.

ecosystems can thrive. Due to deforestation, mining and intensive agriculture, large swathes of the planet are no longer able to sustain stable ecosystems and species that often directly depend on them are disappearing. Even when it is not so much a matter of depletion but of changed use, such as the construction of ports in coastal areas or the building of cities, habitats and eventually species disappear. The fragmentation of larger areas into ever smaller ones is an additional negative effect of increased building activity in (the periphery of) urban areas. Climate change caused by industry and mobility is also putting ecosystems under pressure. While it is true that most ecosystems are able to respond to these changes, they cannot do so as fast as the climate is currently changing. Evolution, both of species and of ecosystems, is a slow process compared to the speed at which climate change is currently taking place. In that respect, there is too little time for adaptation. Moreover, because of industry, including agribusiness and agriculture, and our consumption behaviour, there is extensive pollution and even poisoning of the earth. This too leads to the disappearance of species.
All these factors and their consequences are taking place more or less simultaneously and all across the globe. Several ecosystems are probably already past their tipping point, making rebound impossible and their collapse a real threat. Quite apart from the ethical question of whether we humans have the right to deny existence to plants and animals, our behaviour also hurts ourselves and equally threatens our own livelihood.

People and Nature
To deal with these problems, we will have to relate to nature in a different way than we have done so far. The exploitation of the planet has reached its limits. The first human settlements arose partly as protection from 'wild' nature. Our homes were primarily designed to protect us from climatic influences. And our activities consisted of obtaining food and resources from nature. Humankind placed itself above nature. We tellingly called the parts not yet cultivated by us 'wilderness' waiting to be modified and used in our agricultural system. It is not so long ago that we also began to position ourselves as guardians of some parts of nature, protecting landscapes and natural areas. But still this position 'alongside' nature assumes that humans and their activities are 'different' and superior to those of the other representatives of life.

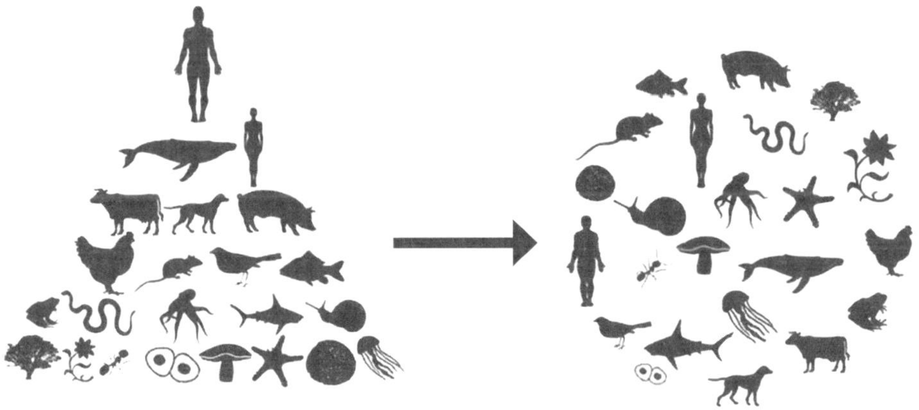

Nature-inclusive building requires a change: from an anthropocentric attitude to an ecocentric one, in which humans are not the only deciding factor.

New climate and nature thinkers are making varying calls to change this basic attitude towards nature. We need to start realizing that we are inextricably linked to nature, and that our presence and actions are utterly intertwined with the life systems around us. If we weaken those systems, we weaken ourselves; if we exploit them, we exploit ourselves. The idea that humans are opposite to or apart from nature is outdated. It directly endangers our own survival. The assumption that 'people use nature to live' is better replaced by inclusive notions such as people living 'with nature', 'as nature' or 'in nature'. We need to change our anthropocentric attitude to an ecocentric one. We live together with all plants and animals – not beside them – on a planet that has its obvious limits. Only together can we find our way out of these problems. Recent discussions speak of a need for a 'Symbiocene', a system beyond the Anthropocene, balancing humans and their technology with nature.

A technological leap forward in which we solve problems 'our way', for instance by synthetically producing food and genetically 'improving' species (whether or not they are on the verge of extinction) may temporarily mitigate the problems, but it can never be the only solution. After all, at best we would end up with a completely synthetic world. But chances are that somewhere along the way we will make another mistake and only exacerbate the problems.

This is not to say that we propose to completely submit to nature from now on. As humanity, we also face a high degree of economic and social inequality. Our purely growth-based economy has brought well-being and prosperity to some parts of the world, but at the expense of the population and ecology of other parts. We can no longer afford such a growth-based economy. If we want to reduce inequalities with regard to prosperity, health and education, it will require an economic system that no longer relies on growth leading to depletion and ecological impoverishment, but on a balance between socio-economic values on the one hand and ecological ones on the other.

What Can We Do?

So, all things considered, the planet faces a huge task. First and foremost, we must stop further degradation of existing ecosystems. We can no longer afford to clear

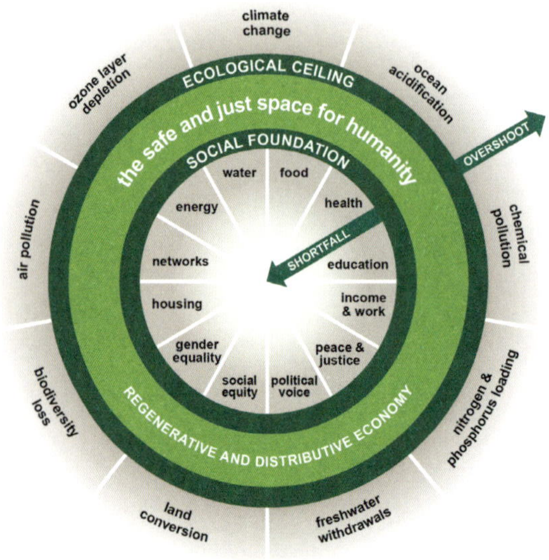

The doughnut diagram describes an economy in which the footprint remains below the ecological ceiling and the impact for people is above the social foundation. This concept, introduced in 2017 by Kate Raworth, combines a socially just world with the long-term preservation of our environment.

land for mining, agriculture and industry. Existing areas have to be preserved and, if possible, restored and expanded. Fragmentation needs to be counteracted, and connections between habitats strengthened or newly created. In addition, areas that have been taken from nature over time, or at least seriously impoverished ecologically, will need to be restored as much as possible. An example of this is so-called 'rewilding', in which habitats are restored, new habitats created and sometimes disappearing original species reintroduced. In agricultural areas, it may also mean developing buffer areas aimed at soil and water restoration, and at creating habitats for a diversity of plants and animals. Other types of agriculture will have to switch to a system that no longer degrades nature, but actually improves it. At the same time, climate change, which includes desiccation and warming and habitat loss from increased wildfires, must also be curbed by moving away from fossil fuels to alternative forms of generating energy.

While the city is firstly the habitat of humans, it is equally a self-contained ecosystem with high biodiversity and many, albeit often fragmented, habitats. Some species have even adapted to the city to such an extent that they cannot live without it.
The need for a more ecological design of public spaces in our cities is now increasingly recognized. Municipalities are hiring ecologists, establishing an ecological network and increasingly focusing on natural management of public green spaces. Buildings also play a role in this process. They represent a large part of our stony city and form its vertical dimension. In some cities, nature-inclusive construction is encouraged or even mandated. But working with nature on and around buildings is trickier than in the streets and parks. And it may also be less self-evident. For why should we give nature a place on buildings? Isn't it enough to design public spaces for this? Parks, canals, road verges, railway viaducts, harbour basins and the like together cover much more area, plus there is a 'real', living soil there that

The Öko-Häuser (eco-houses) project was designed by architect Frei Otto in close cooperation with residents. As part of the International Building Exhibition Berlin 1984/87, it is an example of Ökologisches Bauen (green building) in 1980s Germany. (Frei Otto, 1989-1991, D)

On the scale of the city green structures can be labelled as: green belt, green wedges, concentric, grid and web structure.

is missing on buildings, right? But there are plenty of arguments for designing our buildings nature-inclusively from now on as well.

If people and nature are so inextricably intertwined, then, in relation to animals and to the planet as a whole, it is morally irresponsible and, in the long run, dangerous for ourselves as well, to shirk responsibility as far as our cities and buildings are concerned. Restoring and improving the ecology of both cities and the countryside is an integral task that spans multiple social policy areas, across all scales and in all areas where humans intervene in the ecological system. Architecture cannot and should not shy away from this responsibility.

In densely populated cities, space for nature is rapidly running out. Cities play an ever-greater role in the ecological system and in preserving biodiversity. But also in cities, space at ground level is limited. If we want to boost the green surface in cities, buildings can no longer be exempt from it. Buildings are an integral part of the city's ecological system anyway. Animals use our buildings for nesting and shelter, and plants also thrive if given the space to do so. These animals have found opportunities in the ledges, cracks and crevices of our older buildings, and have adapted to urban life. However, new construction methods have increasingly diminished these spaces. Animals and plants were not included as users in their own right, weakening the city's ecological system.

A single building is generally not capable of maintaining a full-fledged biotope.

The building and the ecology of its immediate surroundings will always need to be mutually complementary and adaptive, and similarly interact with the ecological structure of the city as a whole. Buildings play their own role in this structure: they

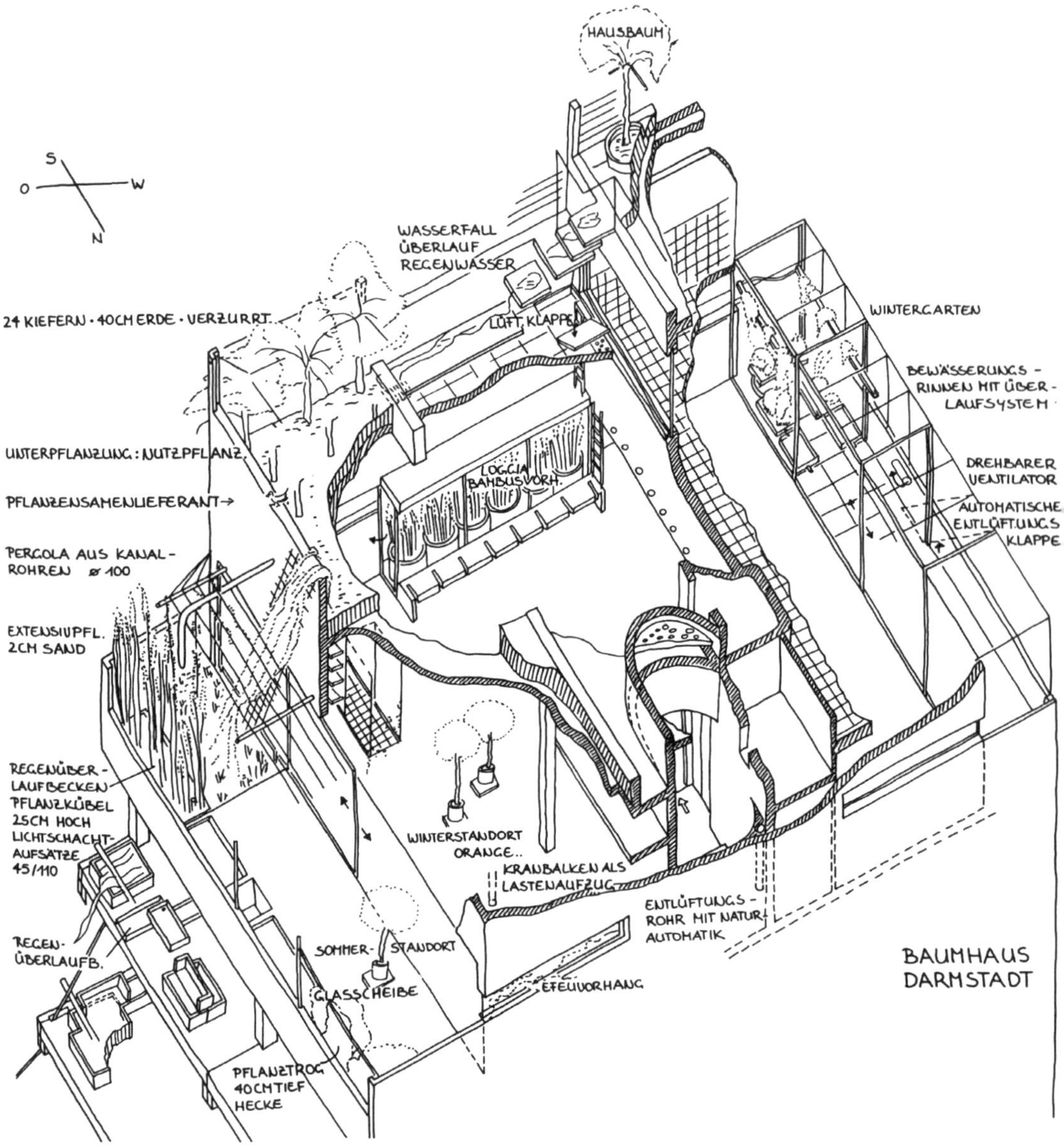

The water management system and the planting form a coherent whole in the Baumhaus. As Hoffmann spent a lot of time in the wild, he knew how to be self-supporting. In his own house he pioneered with autarkic techniques of his own invention. (Ot Hoffmann, 1968-1972, D)

are the 'rock formations' along the valleys of our streets and parks. If from now on we invite plants and animals to the facades and roofs of our buildings, a huge potential of new green surfaces in the city will be created. In other words, buildings play a role in the ecosystem. And we also get something in return. Because nature provides a number of essential services. In cities, these mainly involve capturing particulate matter, reducing heat stress and regulating water management. But we also enjoy nature. A city without nature is also an unlivable city for people.

In cities, flooding poses a pressing problem. Climate change and subsidence play a part in this.

Biodiversity stripes diagrams show how biodiversity is evolving. Green represents high diversity, grey low diversity. With the many shades of colour from full green, through yellow to dark grey, trends are revealed. This diagram shows trends worldwide. From 1970 to 2018, biodiversity has declined by 69 per cent / The climate warming stripes for the period from 1901 to 2020 illustrate how our climate is changing. The colour of the dashes shows the average temperature per year: blue represents relatively cool years, and red warmer years.

Finally, inviting nature onto our buildings requires a fundamentally different design attitude. No longer nature-proof, but nature-inclusive. Buildings that no longer cause problems, but solve them. Because we have to, but also because it is challenging and exciting to take this new path in architecture. This book is above all intended as a guide and inspiration to explore this new path in architecture that can contribute to a beautiful, pleasant and above all natural city of the future.

Planetary Boundaries

The Stockholm Resilience Centre has been investigating the state of our planet's ecological boundaries from the perspective of nine 'planetary life support systems' since 2007. In 2009, the results were first summarized in a diagram showing in red when the boundary of a 'safe operating space for humanity' has been crossed. Updates followed in 2015 and 2022-23.

In the 2009 version, some sectors could not yet be quantified. With the publication of the latest update in September 2023, the figures and their impact on the environment for all nine systems studied were published for the first time. And the message has not become any more reassuring over the past 14 years. In addition to nitrogen and phosphorus issues and intensified climate change, biodiversity loss has long passed the safety threshold.

The institute has been translating biodiversity as 'biosphere integrity' since the 2015 version and it is divided into two parts: genetic and functional diversity. The first part (genetic) describes the alarmingly high rate of species disappearance. The second part (functional) describes the impact of this loss on different ecosystems; it is a measure of the health of these ecosystems. This therefore also affects the ecosystem services that nature provides to us. An example is that a decrease in the number of birds can lead to an increase in insects, which can cause damage to trees and thus mean less CO_2-storage.

The diagram titles of most of the systems studied speak for themselves. Novel Entities concerns the increase of previously unknown chemicals in the atmosphere, soil and water, whose impact on 'planetary life support systems' in the future is currently unknown. However, the quantity is already being interpreted as 'beyond the safe operating space'.

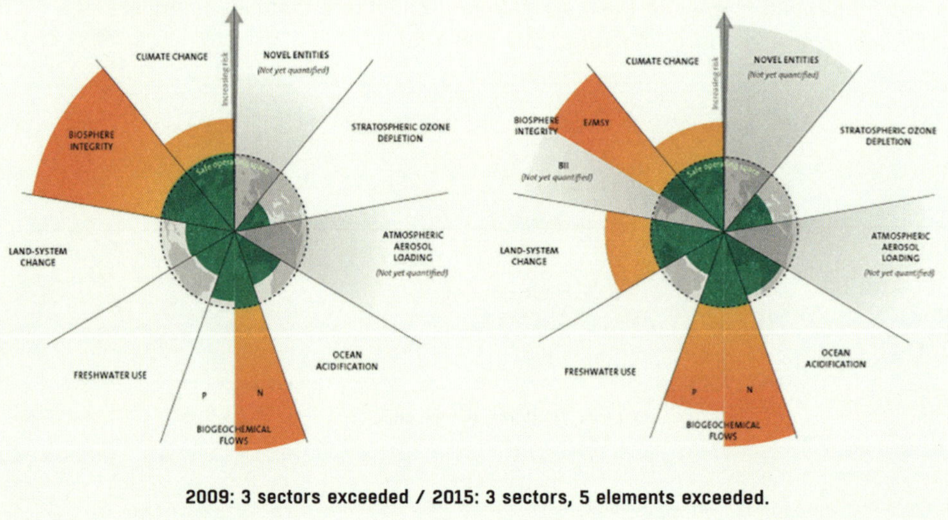

2009: 3 sectors exceeded / 2015: 3 sectors, 5 elements exceeded.

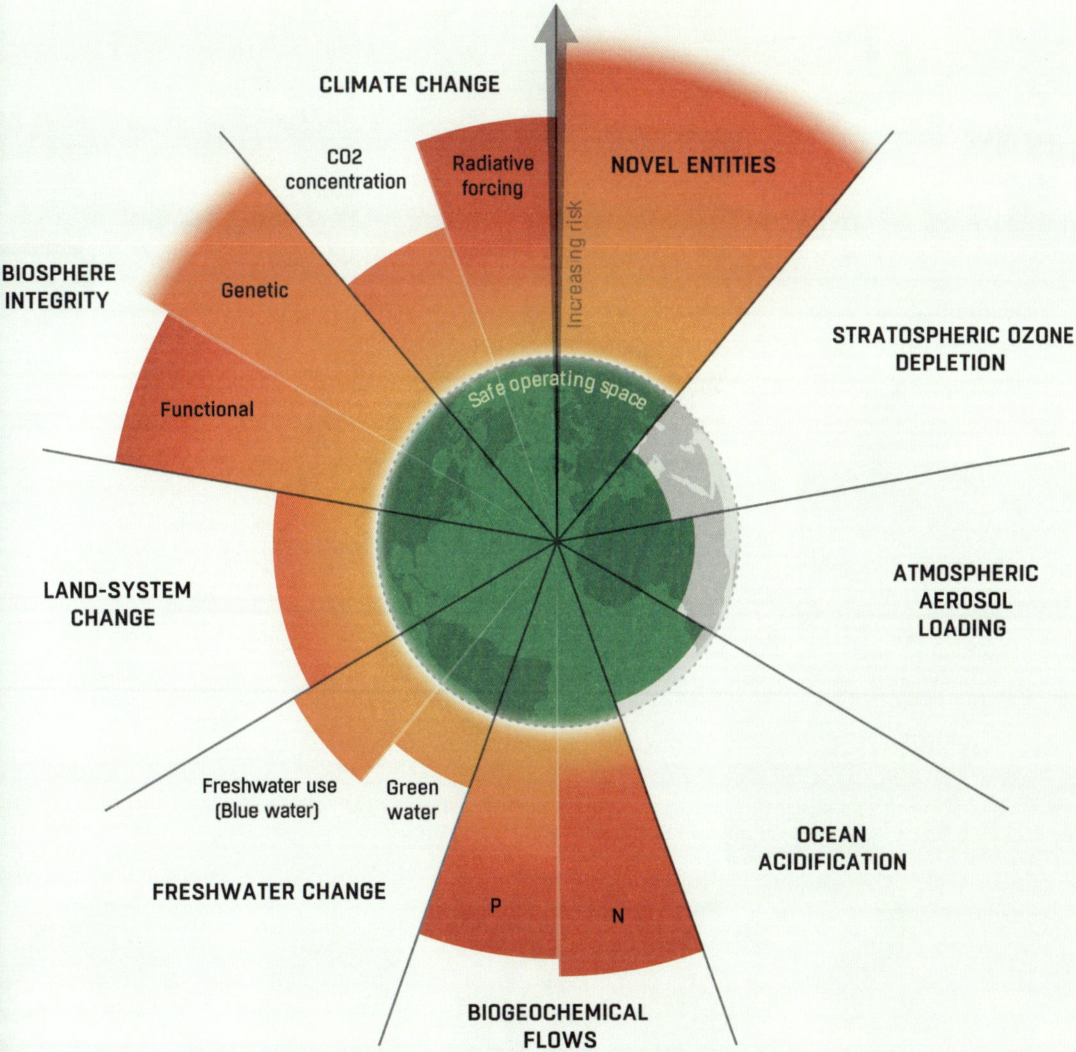

2023: 6 sectors, 10 elements exceeded.

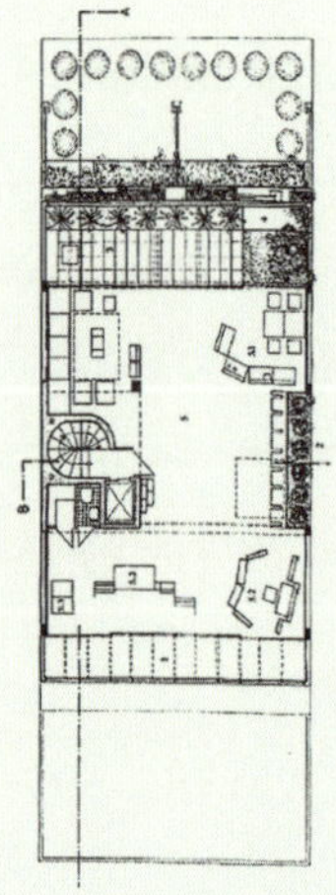

Baumhaus

Darmstadt, Ot Hoffmann, 1968-1972, D

Architect Ot Hoffmann was a pioneer within the ecological architecture movement in Germany in the 1970s. He translated his ideal into the design for his own residence in downtown Darmstadt. The residence, atop offices with a gallery on the ground floor, has vegetated terraces that provide shelter for a colony of sparrows and other birds. The large projections at the front are the start of a bridge to the park across the street that was never realized.

Hoffmann built the Baumhaus (tree house) as part of an urban design he created but which never came to be. A residential street was supposed to connect the new construction of several residential buildings on the first floor. The Herrngarten would serve as an entrance area from which the dwellings would be accessible via a bridge. The roof terraces have been given the same amount of greenery as the area of the ground surface on which the building stands. A few large pines stand out. On a trip to Scandinavia, Hoffmann had seen pine trees growing in a thin layer of earth on the underlying rocks. Therefore, the roof terraces are planted with pine trees, between which shrubs and trees have spontaneously established themselves over time. The balconies projecting over the road are fitted with containers for trees and shrubs.

According to Hoffmann, materials such as loam and traditional grass roofs could not be used for construction in the city centre. These construction techniques were not suitable for compact multi-storey buildings, in Hoffmann's opinion, so he opted for an innovative concrete building system. A waterproof concrete structure was used for the flat roofs. The main challenge was to prevent cracking due to expansion and contraction. This was done through the composition of the concrete, by limiting its dimensions and using sliding stays. The watertight concrete roof structure does not need a waterproofing membrane. There is also no vapour barrier, which provides natural humidity regulation. Insulation was applied directly onto the concrete with a filter layer on top.

'The building will have no gutters. Water will simply run off from roof terrace to roof terrace. An ecological balance will eventually develop in the water storage tanks with fish. Planting will find its way by itself.'

Rainwater is directly absorbed by the roof gardens. Excess water is stored in tanks. Water from the household, including grey water from the toilets, is pumped up and cleaned in tanks on the roof and then used as grey water for the vegetation.

Pine tree on cantilevered overhang / Windmill / Solar boiler and shower, part of the gray water system / Original urban planning design / View of roof terrace from the apartment / Freely arrangeable floor plan of apartment / View of backside Baumhaus.

3

How did early humans first learn to build? It's quite possible that it was by observing animals that had already mastered the art. Indeed, when you look at the animal world, many birds, insects and mammals are excellent architects and builders. Social insects such as bees, wasps, ants and termites construct what many have described as the animal equivalents of the cities of humans.

PAUL DOBRASZCZYK

Nature-inclusive Design

Nature-inclusive building is building differently. It requires a different approach to the construction, use and maintenance of particularly facades and roofs. It invites non-human users and adds new functional requirements to the design brief. As such, it also requires a different design attitude from architects.

Originally, the purpose of building houses and settlements was also to keep out nature. A house provided protection from the climate, from rain, wind, cold and heat, but often also from animals considered dangerous or harmful. This attitude gained additional impetus from hygienic motives during the twentieth century. Recently, for reasons of sustainability and energy conservation, our buildings have moreover been stripped of cracks and crannies where animals and sometimes even plants used to find a home. The architecture itself also became smoother, sleeker and cleaner. To a large extent, modern architecture is an anthropocentric, nature-exclusive functionalism. Intentionally and unintentionally, our buildings became sterile and nature-resistant. From a human perspective, this may have been understandable and rational, but it is an attitude we can no longer afford. It is also an unwarranted attitude, as we have been sharing our habitat with plants and animals for centuries. Knowingly in the form of livestock and pets, but also unknowingly, as all kinds of animals take shelter and build nests in structures we make. From barns and houses to churches and ice cellars, from bridges and quay walls to ramparts and chimneys.

A good example of the need to look at our buildings differently is the way we deal with (rain) water. Protection from rain and wind is the primary requirement that we as people place on our buildings. They are therefore constructed in such a way that not a drop of water can get in and the water is drained as quickly as possible. But water is of vital importance for plants and animals. If we want to allow these fellow users into our buildings, we will also have to allow water. Furthermore, the requirement to retain rainwater in our buildings for longer is also made from a climate perspective. In milder climate zones such as north-western Europe, the pressure on the sewage system becomes too great during increasingly heavy rainfall. Instead of building in such a way

'Animal architecture', Daniel Arsham (2010).

On traditional farms humans and animals lived together in the same building.

that the water is drained as quickly as possible, it is better to increase the absorptive capacity of our buildings, streets and squares and drain the water only when there is really too much of it.
Aesthetics are also changing. Today's architecture is compact, smooth, sleek and neat, but that is all of little use to nature. Life cannot settle on an ultra-flat, smooth glass curtain wall, but it can on a porous, uneven facade. A compact building, understandable from an energy conservation point of view, offers nature no points of attachment, no crevices, ledges, edges, recesses or horizontal surfaces on and in which birds can shelter or build their nests, or bats can find a home. Let alone that plants can settle there. This is perceived as messy and 'dirty'. The maintenance of nature-inclusive buildings therefore differs from what we have been used to. A certain amount of messiness must be allowed, at least of what we have come to think of as messy.
Modern architecture is also predictable. We build with the highest possible degree of control for a specific user with specific wishes and requirements. Deviations from the ideal due to weathering or wear are cleaned and repaired. Anticipating changing use would also be sensible for people—and does happen here and there—and is necessary for nature development. Ecology is characterized by the dynamics of resource and energy flows, as well as the interactions, population trends, adaptations and succession of species. So, nature is less predictable.

Of course, this does not mean that from now on we should just make unfinished, unhygienic or leaky and draughty buildings. The aspiration to build more naturally is additional to the need for healthy and sustainable construction. The two requirements

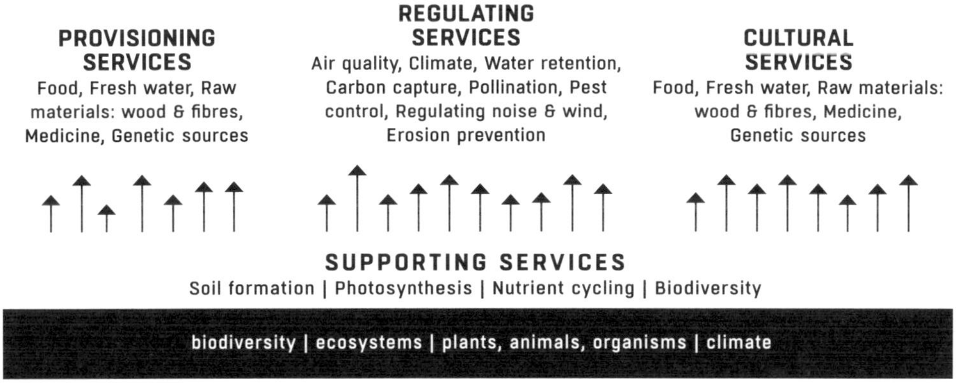

Based on supporting services, nature provides provisioning services, regulating services, and cultural services.

need not be mutually exclusive, in fact, and may even reinforce each other. A green city is a healthy city and a vegetated roof or facade reduces warming and wind nuisance around buildings, thereby (somewhat) reducing cooling and heating demand.
The claim on space in the city is considerable and architects today have to deal with more restrictive regulations than before. So, it is not easy. But it does not help to problematize this. It is more fruitful to see opportunities and challenges in it. After all, the equally difficult requirements of hygiene and sustainability have also led to a new architecture. Why couldn't the same be true for the new requirement of allowing nature onto our buildings? After all, over the course of history, we have also learned to experience that nature in the city is beautiful and even essential for our health and well-being. It would really only be a small step to look at our buildings in the same way from now on.

Apart from the ethical and aesthetic arguments, nature also provides us with functional benefits. Without nature, the city does not function properly. These so-called ecosystem services are different in nature and range from provisioning services, such as providing food and fuel, to cultural services, such as providing recreational opportunities. Unlimited use of these productive and cultural services, however, can lead to depletion. This is not the case for the most important ecosystem services, the so-called regulating services. These involve things that a well-functioning ecosystem 'automatically' provides without running the risk of depletion. In part, these are supporting services, which ensure the functioning of the system itself, such as maintaining a healthy soil life, biodiversity or natural pollination, which, incidentally, is also essential for our food production. But it also involves services that without the natural system could only be provided using extensive technical facilities. Nature's ability to absorb 'excess' water and retain it until dryer times reduces, for example, the need for increased sewerage capacity or the creation of new urban drainage channels. Attenuating heat stress avoids having to install expensive shading or cooling systems. The ability to clean air and water and to counter erosion also reduces the need for often costly technical solutions. Moreover, the presence of nature is beneficial to our health and thus also prevents medical costs. From this perspective, nature has economic value in addition to its

unquestionable intrinsic value. This added value can be calculated with tools such as TEEB-city or i-Tree.
On a larger scale, nature development in the form of so-called 'nature-based solutions' is already being applied as an alternative to purely technical solutions. For example, by creating new nature in large coastal defence projects and in preventing erosion of mountain slopes. The added advantage of these solutions is that 'free' ecosystem services are included, which is not the case with a purely technical solution. Of course, smaller-scale solutions are also conceivable based on the services provided by nature. When working out engineering problems, it should become self-evident to also, in fact first of all, think of such solutions based on the natural system. It can be fruitful to reverse the perspective and not only think in terms of the benefits nature offers us, but also in terms of how nature benefits from our intervention. It is precisely thinking from this reciprocal 'win-win situation' that can be decisive in choosing the best design decision.

Three Design Perspectives

So, a less anthropocentric and more nature-inclusive design requires a modified design and thus a modified design process. First of all, nature—plants and animals—must be included in the brief as an equally important user alongside people. Each design assumes different perspectives with a specific solution-path; the (human) user perspective, the technical perspective, the aesthetic perspective, the historical perspective and the urban planning context. In a good and complete design, all these principles are addressed to a greater or lesser extent and they reinforce each other. Depending on the nature of the design task or the client's request, accents are placed and not every requirement will be met to the same extent. But excluding any of these perspectives or starting points is almost inconceivable. Except for the natural perspective, that is. For that was until recently the 'hobby' of a limited number of ecotects. However, this natural perspective does not replace any of the existing ones, but is additional and equivalent to it. Broadly speaking, there are three ways of looking at this new design task. The systemic perspective: from the ecological system. The biological perspective: from the experience and the wishes and requirements of plants and animals. The architectural perspective: from the appearance and execution of buildings. Of course, these perspectives are also related and especially relevant in their interconnection.

The Systemic Perspective

In nature, everything is interconnected in a complex and dynamic ecosystem. Knowledge of this system in general, and that of a building's immediate environment in particular, is crucial for the viability of interventions. Architects have long been used to including the context of a building in their design. Especially in an urban environment, it is virtually impossible to design completely autonomously. The external historical, urban planning, social and aesthetic context within which a design is created is often as decisive for the final result as the requested function. In terms of the ecological context too, it makes little sense and is even impossible to build completely autonomously. However, unlike for the city as a whole, where maintaining or strengthening an independent ecological structure is a necessity, it is virtually impossible for a solitary

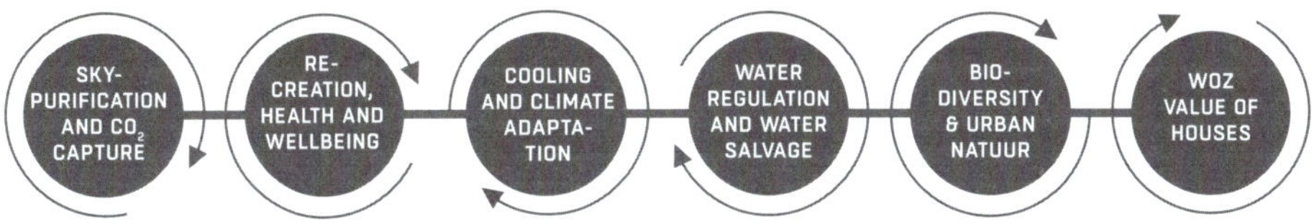

The TEEB City Tool is an online tool that converts ecosystem services into monetary value. The result can give biodiversity a more powerful voice in decision-making.

building in the city to house such a composition and quantity of plants and animals with their own interactions with each other and the abiotic circumstances that a self-sustaining system will emerge. The scale of the building is generally too small for this. But a building can contain elements of an ecosystem, and there will be species that will be able to make do with the building as a habitat, such as a green roof that can function on its own for certain insects or plants. Due to the small scale, though, you cannot see this as its own ecosystem, but only as part of the ecosystem that is the city. The existing ecological structure around the building is therefore taken as a starting point, and the aim is to create a symbiosis where building and environment (living and non-living) work together. Nature-inclusive measures can be aimed at strengthening the urban ecosystem, or adding missing parts to it. Connections to the immediate environment are essential. A bird that finds its food in an adjacent park can nest in the building right next to it because the functions of safety, reproduction and food are located in close proximity. Plants from a roof garden can be pollinated by insects from the surrounding area and vice versa. A green facade or a roof garden can play an essential role as a stepping stone in the city's ecological connections. There is little point in installing a nesting box for house sparrows when there are no shrubs or hedges in the immediate vicinity. And when bat boxes hang somewhere with a lot of artificial light, bats will never move in. Abiotic factors such as wind and therefore dry conditions on taller buildings also determine whether a measure makes sense or not. In short: a building and how it functions in relation to biodiversity is never isolated from its surroundings. In the larger system, it will mainly function as a stepping stone, as an intermediate step when species move from one area to another.

For the design of Vertical in Amsterdam Sloterdijk, future biotopes were mapped. This served as the basis for determining what architectural features were to be applied. (Vertical, DS landschapsarchitecten, 2016, NL)

Every architect is, to a greater or lesser extent, a generalist and has sufficient knowledge of the different perspectives to merge them all equally. With the increased complexity of the building process, all kinds of consultants have joined the architect, adding specialist sub-knowledge to the basics: the structural engineer, the mechanical engineer, the building cost expert, et cetera. A certain basic ecological knowledge and understanding of the opportunities and possibilities of the natural environment is important, but just as a design of the load-bearing structure is no longer possible without the help of a structural engineer, the involvement of an (urban) ecologist is necessary when designing a well-functioning ecosystem on and around the building.

The Biological Perspective

Needless to say, the city is not originally the primary natural habitat of wild plants and animals. And a building made especially for humans least of all. Yet nature thrives in our cities and our buildings. Urban biodiversity is often greater than the sometimes agriculture- and industry-dominated countryside. Some species have adapted to living in cities and buildings to such an extent that they have become 'city-bound' and have come to use the city as their natural habitat. The city also offers many advantages for species that can cope with the dynamics of the city. It is often warmer there than in surrounding areas. It is safer for some species because many natural predators are absent (though in the city, they face other predators, such as dogs and domestic cats). It can be healthier because much less (agricultural) toxins are used (though in the city, there is more air pollution) and there is more variety and supply of food and opportunities to shelter and breed for all kinds of species. If you look at the city from the perspective of plants and animals, you do not see a collection of human nests, but a landscape in which the buildings and the streets in between present themselves as cliffs with valleys, rivers and groves in between. Nature basically makes no distinction between this artificial landscape of the city and the 'real' landscape outside, as long as the conditions for settlement are favourable.

This biological perspective, to look at the 'landscape' qualities of a building through the eyes of animals and plants, can be both generic and specific. Are the general characteristics of the building's shape and execution of roof and facade such that passing birds could see a rock wall in it? For a smooth-faced block, this is probably not the case. On steep, smooth rock faces, there is also little life to be found. With a stepped facade with, for example, planters, there is a greater chance of settlement or at least of providing a resting place or foraging area. A building's generic landscape qualities invite nature without having a specific target species in mind. But sometimes there may be a need from the environment to help a specific species. For example, a sparrow colony in the street may need more nesting opportunities. In such cases, it is primarily a functional question, such as either built-in or exterior nesting boxes of a size and design suitable for sparrows. But even then, it is good to keep in mind the more general characteristics of a habitat and of the natural behaviour of house sparrows, such as bushes or hedges very close to the building. If house sparrows accept the environment as 'natural', there is a good chance that other species will do the same. From the biological perspective, the presence of such 'indicator species' means it is almost certain that it is a suitable habitat for other species as well.

The Architectural Perspective

We can also look at the nature-inclusive task from an architectural perspective; at formal qualities and the main shape of the building. From an urban planning perspective, for example, the ecosystem of the city as a whole can be seen as a system of planes (the parks and larger public gardens), lines (the ecological connections in the form of roadsides, rows of trees or canals) and points (the more isolated, smaller habitats that can function as stepping stones in the bigger picture). Practically speaking, the planes and lines can only be realized on an urban scale. But from the biological perspective, as described earlier, buildings are inseparable from the points, the stepping stones in the ecological infrastructure. This interconnectedness is what makes it possible for the urban ecosystem to function.

With buildings, it is about the chosen overall shape or the specific additions to, for example, roof or facade. The choice of the overall shape of the building determines the options for connecting with the surrounding ecological network.

Not coincidentally, given the biological perspective, buildings with a landscape-like shape are the most obvious example of this. A terraced shape that rises from the ground level to the roof, with the terraces and roof being vegetated, presents itself as a hilly landscape and for that reason alone offers more prospects for effective nature-inclusive measures. But such buildings also require more space, the ratio between the required foot print and the total usable area is less favourable (especially economically) and therefore not always feasible. But even a compact block or tower can be made nature-inclusive by adding natural building components to the facade, roof or base of the building.

The city's green-blue network can be divided into four main components. The green hubs are large-scale parks and lakes. These are interconnected by green-blue lines along canals, roads and other urban infrastructure. A chain of smaller green public spaces can also serve as connecting elements. From this main urban structure, branching lines pierce the densely built-up central area. Within this network of lines and surfaces are the islands, such as neighbourhood parks and green roofs.

The facade in particular, but also the roof of a building, has to meet a range of functional requirements: providing protection from cold, rain and wind, providing views and daylighting, the means to ventilate and—a recent addition—if possible generating energy through solar panels. In this respect, nature-inclusive aspirations have to compete with these structural, physical and functional requirements. But competition is not the right word, it is about addition; ecological requirements are added to the already existing ones. The outer shell of a facade in particular can provide opportunities for this. Is there a cavity or are there gaps where animals can shelter? Is the material porous or uneven? Are there ledges or surfaces where plants can settle?

The facade can also be stretched into a residential interior by adding intermediate spaces such as balconies, pergolas and atriums. The intermediate space thus created can accommodate urban flora and fauna in addition to residential space for human occupants; a space where people and nature meet. Such a transition zone between outdoor space and human-inhabited, air-conditioned indoor space also has an attenuating effect on undesirable climate effects; for example, it reduces wind nuisance around the building as well as excessive heating.

The Nature-inclusive Design Process

Nature-inclusive design and construction is not yet self-evident and is currently still in the pioneering phase. Knowledge and experience are not always sufficiently present or at least unevenly distributed among the various parties participating in the construction process. It is therefore wise to agree with all parties involved (municipality, client, users, builders, consultants and designers) right at the start of the design process what the ambitions are with regard to incorporating nature in the design. An ecologist can help at this stage with questions such as: which ecological values do we want to preserve or add? In what way do we connect to the local ecological quality? Are there specific species we want to accommodate? Are there

ecosystem services we want to call on? Don't think of these principles as a possible option, but as conditions. Lay them down in the design brief and safeguard them up to the final design. Include maintenance after completion, as this is a vulnerable phase in which, for instance, greenery needs care to reach maturity.
Apart from the question of what measures will be taken, it is also advisable to collectively discuss the reasons for taking these measures. These may be pragmatic, because the Nature Conservation Law or local regulations demand it, or to meet set climate goals. But more important is the intrinsic motivation; the realization that buildings also contribute to urban ecology and the preservation of biodiversity and thus to the realization of a more beautiful and healthier city, both for people and for plants and animals.

Principles

The process starts with determining the ecological values and potentials of the site. A city centre street is a different biotope from a residential area on the outskirts of the municipality. Make an inventory of the species present and determine whether and what additional measures can boost local ecology. Sometimes a municipality already has a green structure map or a map with (desired and present) ecological connections or a memorandum in which target species, icon species, indicator species or whatever they are called, are designated as species that deserve extra attention in the municipality.
Therefore, you should always ask the question: on the construction site, are there perhaps 'hiatuses' in the present ecology? Plants or animals that belong there but do not live there yet or are no longer there? As far as possible, do this together with an (urban) ecologist. Also involve local nature enthusiasts in this research. They often know which plants and animals are already there and which species are native/local, and which ones could use a boost. Establish which place the building occupies in the larger ecological system of the city and how it can contribute to strengthening the green and blue networks. But also the brown networks (soil) if there is knowledge about them, and certainly also the black networks (light/dark) to ensure that no more lighting is used than necessary. A building on the perimeter of an ecological zone has different requirements and possibilities than an isolated building in an environment with hardly any possibilities for connection. If the latter is the case, the building should be developed primarily as a stepping stone in the larger network, mainly for birds and, to a lesser extent, insects.
Also observe the interaction between the various species. How are they interrelated? If this coherence is disrupted by construction, for example because an essential link in the cycle or food web disappears, assess how this disruption can be remedied. But be realistic about the possibilities. It makes little sense, for example, to install nest boxes for specific bird species if these species are currently nowhere to be found in the area. Strengthening existing values often has the most potential. Generally, however, measures will be generic in nature and make a general contribution. Perhaps other birds will breed in those 'superfluous' nest boxes. In this phase, it is mainly a matter of finding, on the one hand, specific measures that are necessary or useful and, on the other, generic measures that always work and contribute one way or the other.

Design site analysis involves more than mapping the green network (including trees, roadsides, parks, and allotments) and the blue network (including canals, ditches, ponds and lakes). The brown network, or soil with its inestimable amount of hidden biodiversity, and the black network of dark and lit areas are equally important. Artificial light, for instance, has a significant impact on the lives of not only plants and animals, but also of people.

Nature-inclusive Measures

The elaboration of this 'natural' part of the brief is a matter of (building) technology *and* architecture. Specific nature-inclusive building components, materials and detailing principles can be inserted, but if these are applied as mere additions, they can easily be cut out again. When asked how he justified the extra cost of green measures to his buildings, French architect Edouard François replied: 'When you take away the green stuff, my buildings look like shit. The green stuff ís the architecture.' This is a shining example of how we should look at nature-inclusive architecture.

Look for 'nature-based solutions'; measures that not only have ecological value, but also provide other benefits, such as mitigating wind nuisance or heat-stress or adding extra spaces for the users of the building, such as 'green' terraces and patios.

Nature-inclusive construction is not free, but it does not have to be expensive either if the measures are specified early on and integrated into the design. Include the added value of ecosystem services in that economic consideration. At what level is the measure likely to generate savings, for instance because the absorption of rainwater reduces the cost of rainwater drainage?

Cocreation and Communication

Nature-inclusive design is a new discipline. Communication with all stakeholders is necessary to avoid misunderstandings. Explain why nature-inclusive building is important. Address the benefits for people and nature, as well as the collective responsibility of users in subsequent management. It will increase enthusiasm and may overcome any resistance. Gain support by collectively weighing up which measures are useful and desirable. Involving users and builders in the design will create understanding and

A housing project initiated by the residents themselves. Improving biodiversity is one of the design principles. Native plants in containers on the facade, on the roof terrace and in the courtyard garden are integral to the grey-water system as rich biotopes. (De Warren, Amsterdam, Natrufied, 2023, NL)

moreover can help find new solutions. Perhaps some residents would like to take on part of the maintenance? And with many measures to benefit nature, there is also choice: there are several plant species suitable for a green roof to provide value for birds and insects, for example, so residents in this example can also choose what they themselves like or enjoy within that palette.

Realization and Management

The construction process itself disturbs wildlife in the area and may therefore also be a factor in the eventual success. Animals driven away by construction activities might not return. So don't chase away future natural residents. During demolition and new construction, provide 'temporary housing' at the shortest possible distance for animals living in the existing building. For protected species, this is already a statutory rule (mitigating measures). Avoid activities that disturb local nature during construction. Think, for instance, about how to minimize light and noise pollution or how to physically protect the trees and plants present. But also think about soil compaction or excavation: respect this 'brown' structure too, so that soil life is preserved as much as possible around the building. And above all: make sure that after the construction process, a higher quality is created than there was before. Nature-inclusive building always provides a 'plus'.

TERRACED HOUSES: Suburbs are characterized by low-rise buildings with mainly ground-level housing. Privately owned houses with a wide variety of gardens allow for rich biodiversity. Measures such as facade greenery and green roofs that homeowners can introduce are also certainly effective when you add them up—albeit on a small scale. (Grasdachsiedlung Laher Wiese, Hannover, 1984/1985, D)

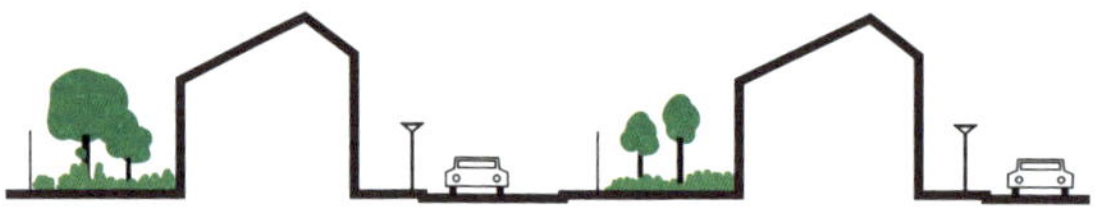

Nature on and attached to buildings usually needs maintenance. Draw up a maintenance protocol and management plan for this, and reserve a budget for implementation. Especially in larger projects, this maintenance and management will have to be done by a professional party (if only for the maintenance of watering systems), but it is a good idea to involve the residents/users as well. This will increase support and participation. Ecology is a dynamic process and only predictable to a limited extent. Plants and animals are constantly adapting to changing conditions. Some plants or animals one had hoped for may not come and live somewhere, while others will do so unplanned. Above all, take your time and allow nature to develop step by step. Accept any failures; they may be accompanied by unexpected successes over time. Monitor development and adjust management and maintenance accordingly in the interim. Monitoring is thus an integral part of the management plan, but also important as a learning opportunity for future projects. Many nature-inclusive measures are in the pioneering phase. To learn what works and what does not, monitoring and publishing about it is essential. Knowledge sharing on specific techniques in relation to the species that settle there is the only way to move the field forward.

COMMUNAL INNER COURTYARD SPACE: Structuring inner courtyards as collective gardens creates opportunities for robust green structures with, for example, a central pond and fully-fledged stands of trees. A sharp contrast with the usual subdividing of inner courtyards into small private lots, which results in fragmentation, also because of fences that go down into the soil. (The Groene Mient, The Hague, Francois Verhoeven, Dennis Fillié and Dennis Hofman, 2020, NL)

THE (INNER-CITY) RESIDENTIAL STREET: Another type of inner-city communal space stems from the restructuring of streets into residential streets, often initiated by residents. Especially when streets are redesigned as low-traffic areas, this offers opportunities for added nature. (Tuinstraat, Lange Riddersstraat, Municipality of Antwerp, 2021, B)

Protected or threatened?

Many animals and plants have the status of 'protected' or 'threatened', and in many cases both. However, there is a difference between these terms. 'Protected' refers to a legal status established by legislation. 'Threatened' is a classification used in science to indicate the status of a species. The 'threatened' status is not always legally secured, which means that the species in question is not 'protected'.

Protection of plants and animals is safeguarded at the European level in the Birds Directive and the Habitats Directive, complemented by the Bern Convention and the Bonn Convention. This not only designates areas but also individual species. All member states are obliged to adhere to these and include them in national legislation, with different countries subsequently allowed to add species of their own based on national concerns. In relation to species that use buildings, this includes all bat species and all birds that return year-round for their nests (such as the house sparrow and common swift) including the roost (whether the animals are currently there or not), with in addition the protection of all birds during the breeding season (only at that time). There are no building-bound plant species with European legal protection.

Threatened plants and animals get this status by being placed on the Red List. These lists are made periodically, both internationally by the IUCN and nationally. However, a Red List has no legal status. Many legally protected species are also on the Red List, but even that is not necessary. There is no direct link between protected and threatened; the terms should be used side by side.

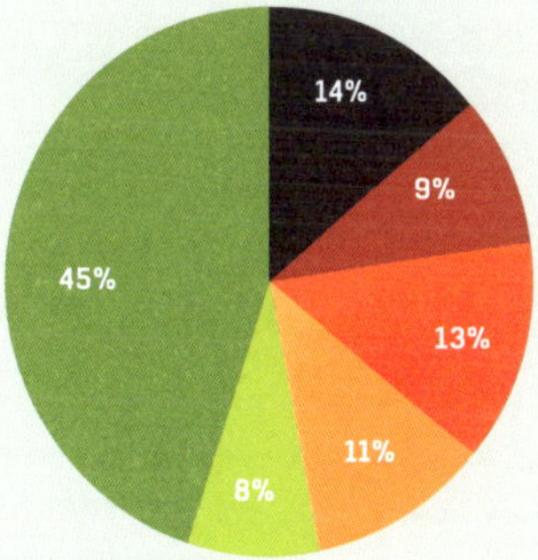

181 species of bees are on the Red List.
That is 55% of the number of species considered

- **Disappeared (VN): 46 species**
- **Critically Endangered (EB): 30 species**
- **Endangered (BE): 42 species**
- **Vulnerable (KW): 38 species**
- **Sensitive (GE): 25 species**
- **Currently not endangered (TNB): 150 species**

Left: Violet-winged mining bee. Very rare and on the Red List as 'vulnerable', but not legally protected. Rustyback. Very rare and on the Red List of vascular plants as 'vulnerable' and is also legally protected.

Nature-inclusive typology

The main shape of a building determines the nature and extent of possible nature-inclusive measures. In order to facilitate discussion about the interpretation of the main shape during the design process, common combinations of shape and function have been described in typologies such as office towers, terrace buildings, *doorzonwoningen* with through lounges and patio houses. If only the shape is considered, tower, terrace building, strip building and the closed building block are used as morphological typologies. Specific nature-inclusive measures can be taken for each of these types. As with all typological classifications, in the end many buildings turn out to be hybrid forms.

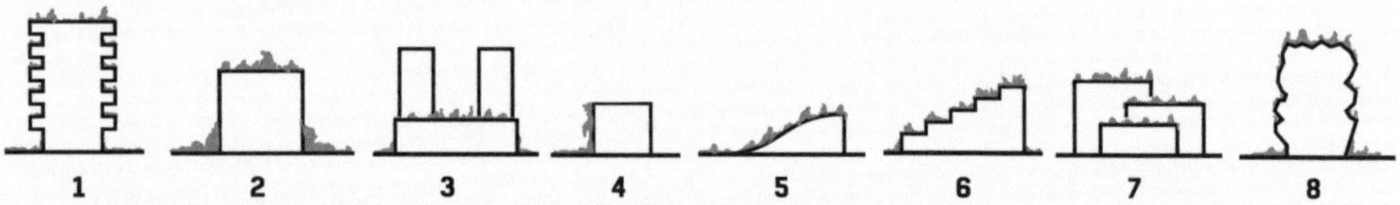

1. TOWER: The facade surface of a tower can be provided with green structures, either through climbing greenery from the base or by adding balconies with plant or tree containers (and combinations). The possibilities on the roof are usually limited due to the small surface area, also because space for installations is needed on the roof.

2. LIFTED GROUND LEVEL: The land taken up by the building is compensated by 'greenery' on the roof. Such roofs are among the most common examples of nature-inclusive buildings, both in inner-city areas, where they serve as stepping stones in the main ecological structure, and on the urban fringes and in the countryside, where they connect to the surrounding nature.

3. LIFTED LANDSCAPE: Similar to the lifted ground level, but halfway up the building. For high-rise buildings, this offers the advantage that the distance from the greenery around the building to the roof gardens is limited. The intermediate garden can connect the ground level with the higher roof gardens.

4. VERTICAL LANDSCAPE: The landscape surrounding the building is continued in a green facade. The base of the building and the facade are merged. This typology is applied where the context provides space for greenery at ground level directly around the building.

5. LANDSCAPE ACROSS THE BUILDING: The building is submerged beneath the landscape. Nature can easily find its way up. This typology is mainly applied outside inner-city areas because it takes up a relatively large amount of space.

6. TERRACE BUILDING: The outdoor spaces of the dwellings are terraced. The relatively small height differences facilitate exchanges between species and possibly also of seeds, among the terraces.

7. STEPPING-STONE BUILDING: The building consists of several volumes, each with a roof garden. The height difference between these gardens is bridgeable and allows exchange between green structures.

8. ROCK BUILDING: Constructed from fragments, a large facade and roof area is created. This provides a wide variety of microclimates and thus biotopes.

1. Bosco Verticale, Milan, Stefano Boeri Architetti, 2014, IT / 2. Residential building Groenmarkt, Amsterdam, Ronald Janssen architecten, Bastiaan Jongerius architecten, Buro Harro, 2022, NL / 3. The Standard Hotel, High Line, New York, Ennead, 2009, US

4. House of Axel Ghyssaert, Bruges, A. Ghyssaert 1969 (B) / 5. Biesbosch Museumeiland, Werkendam, Studio Marco Vermeulen, 2015, NL / 6. Residential building Medina, Eindhoven, Neave Brown, 2003, NL

7. Residential and office building Het Platform, Utrecht, VenhoevenCS, 2020, NL / The Valley, Amsterdam, MVRDV, 2022, NL

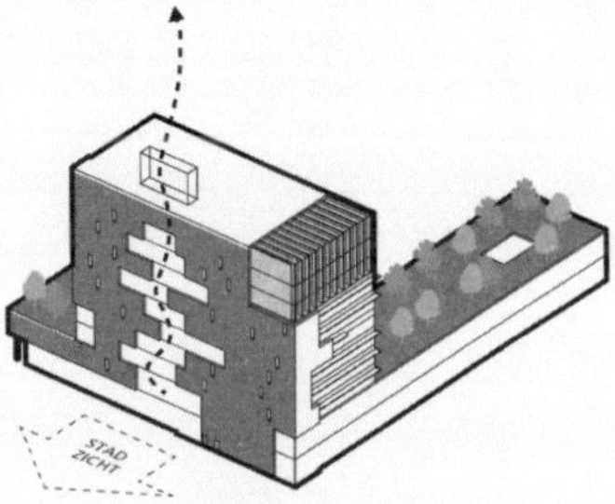

Solar chimney (ventilation by making use of rising warm air).

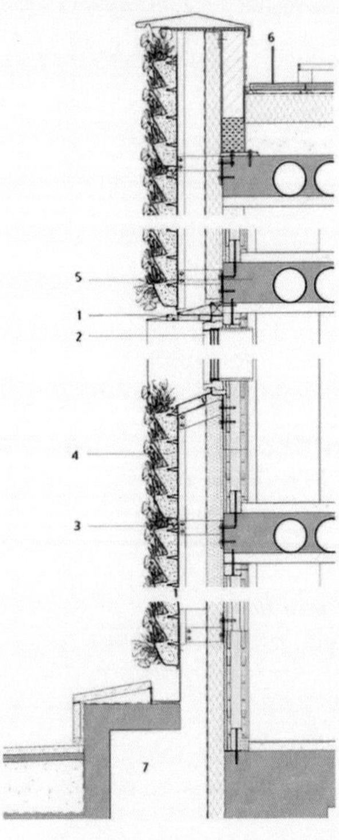

Above: Section living wall.
Left: Greenhouse air supply via roof terrace / Living wall / Patio with water roof / Green facade, provides shelter and nest opportunities for birds.

Stadskantoor Venlo

Kraaijvanger Architects, 2016, NL

Through green facades and roofs, the Venlo city offices building contributes to local biodiversity. The growing system is furthermore designed to provide various ecosystem services. The facade planting is part of the air treatment system. The planting in the atrium is part of the greywater circuit.

The greenhouse with plants on the roof acts as an inlet for ventilation air, while the green facade serves as an air filter for the outgoing air. The greenhouse area also serves as outdoor space for weddings and other festive gatherings. A 'living wall' has been installed with various plant species, including butterfly bushes. An advanced watering system provides the plants with the necessary water and nutrients. The wall acts as a habitat for insects and birds. Feral pigeons have found a home there and, over time, even a peregrine falcon has taken up residence, hunting the pigeons. Maintenance of the planting is largely carried out by machine, except for the places where machines cannot reach.

The grey water from the office is replenished with rainwater and cleaned by reeds and other plants in the ponds in the patio on the roof of the parking garage below.

New buildings with herbaceous roofs have been built behind the building. As a result, the building block, including the city offices building, acts as a stepping stone in Venlo's ecological network.

Roof terrace.

Maggie's Yorkshire

Leeds, Heatherwick Studio, Balston Agius, 2012, GB

Maggie's Centres, founded by Maggie Keswick Jencks (the wife of Charles Jencks) who suffered from cancer and died from it in 1995, are institutions for people dealing with this disease. Complementing medical care, patients, their partners, family members and friends can go there for help and counselling. '*A place where people do not have to lose the joy of living in the fear of dying.*'

For Maggie's Yorkshire in Leeds, greenery was applied as a way to comfort people. Forest plants (shrubs, flowers and trees) typical of Yorkshire were used in the planting of the roof terraces. These plants thrive in the shade of adjacent buildings, the at times strong winds and the northern English climate. The whole forms the basis for biodiversity within a largely stony environment. The interior is also furnished with plants, making it a good example of what is called biophilic design.

The green terraces and interior planting are designed to improve well-being.

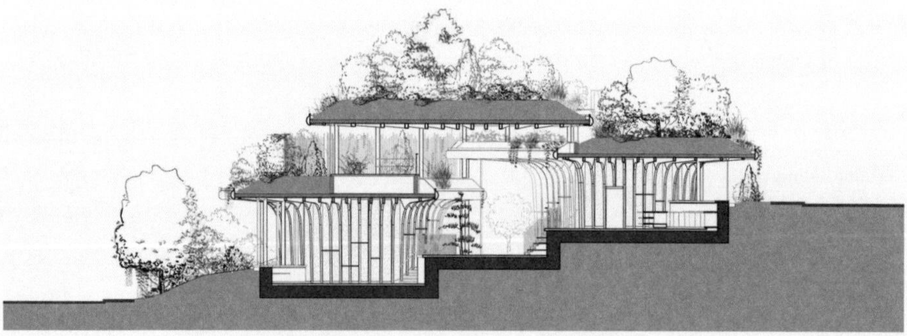

Cross-section.

École des sciences et de la biodiversité

Boulogne-Billancourt, Paris, ChartierDalix, 2014, FR

The municipality of Boulogne-Billancourt launched a competition for a natural learning environment as a green enclave in the highly urbanized city centre. ChartierDalix won the competition with a botanist and an ecologist in the design team. The design is a green learning and playing environment on a building that can be described as an overgrown rock. Around a central playground, classrooms are located on different floors under a terraced roof landscape.

The outer cavity leaf, built up from precast concrete elements, is detailed as a slightly sloping screen, free from the structural, insulated inner wall. The cavity of variable width is accessible to bats, birds and insects. Nest boxes for birds have been integrated into the elevated concrete facade elements. The ends of the lower elements, up to about 3 metres above ground level, have holes in which solitary bees and other insects can nest. The tops of the elements are provided with ridges, in which substrate can collect as a base for the spontaneous growth of mosses and wall plants.

A one-metre strip around the building is unpaved and planted with climbers such as mile-a-minute vine and Virginia creeper. This creates a transitional area between the ground level and the facade. The streets around the project are also partly greened with a water buffering function (wadi).

The building has a number of terraced outdoor spaces with space for a thicket on the highest roof. The thickness of substrate on the roofs varies so that vegetation can be tailored to use. The substrate thickness ranges between 25 and 100 centimetres. With the different soils, three zones were created: a zone with trees (including hornbeams, lime trees, and maples), a zone mainly for shrubs (such as hazel and berry bushes) and a meadow (grasses, leguminous plants and sedum). The vast majority of the gardens are irrigated naturally and the choice was made to allow the planting to evolve with the conditions. The upper part is accessible to students and serves as an outdoor classroom and playground.

Four years after completion, a team of designers and botanists have collected seeds of flowers and herbs around Paris and used them to complement the existing planting. ChartierDalix architects and ecologists are thus working with the school's students, experimenting with seeds and plants both on the facade and on the roof garden to discover what does and does not take root. Maintenance of the roof gardens is a collaborative effort by volunteers and students. Nature development is monitored, and on this basis parts of the roof and its management have been adjusted.

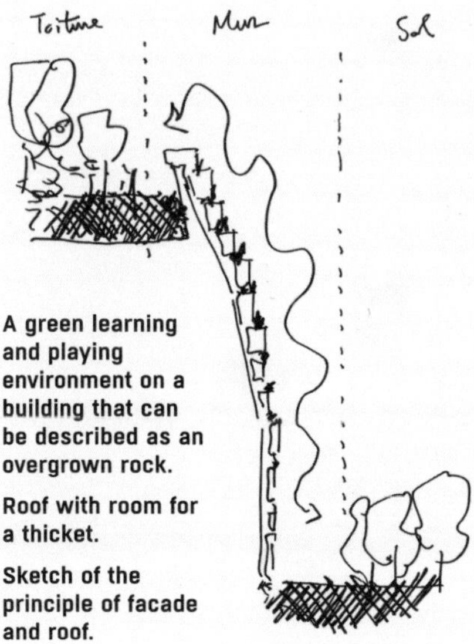

A green learning and playing environment on a building that can be described as an overgrown rock.

Roof with room for a thicket.

Sketch of the principle of facade and roof.

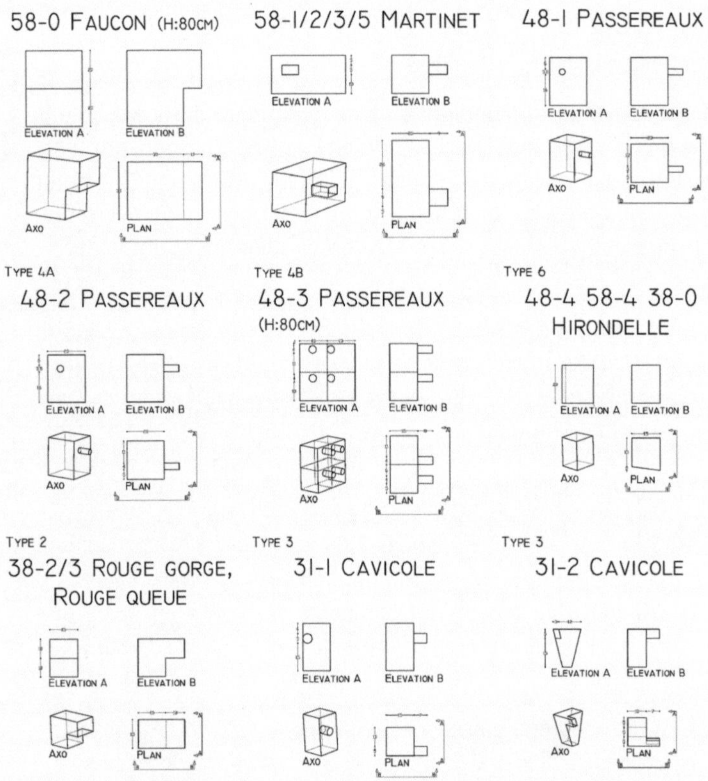

École des sciences et de la biodiversité has nest boxes for birds integrated into the facade elements.

- **(faucon) – kestrel**
- **(martinet) – common swift**
- **(passeraux) – passerine, house sparrow, blue tit, great tit**
- **(hirondelle) – swallow**
- **(rouge gorge) – European robin**
- **(cavicole) – cavity nesters, lesser spotted woodpecker, grass warbler**

Increasing the porosity of the facade was the key design principle. Insects can nest here or plants can take root. Higher up there are nesting boxes for bats and birds.

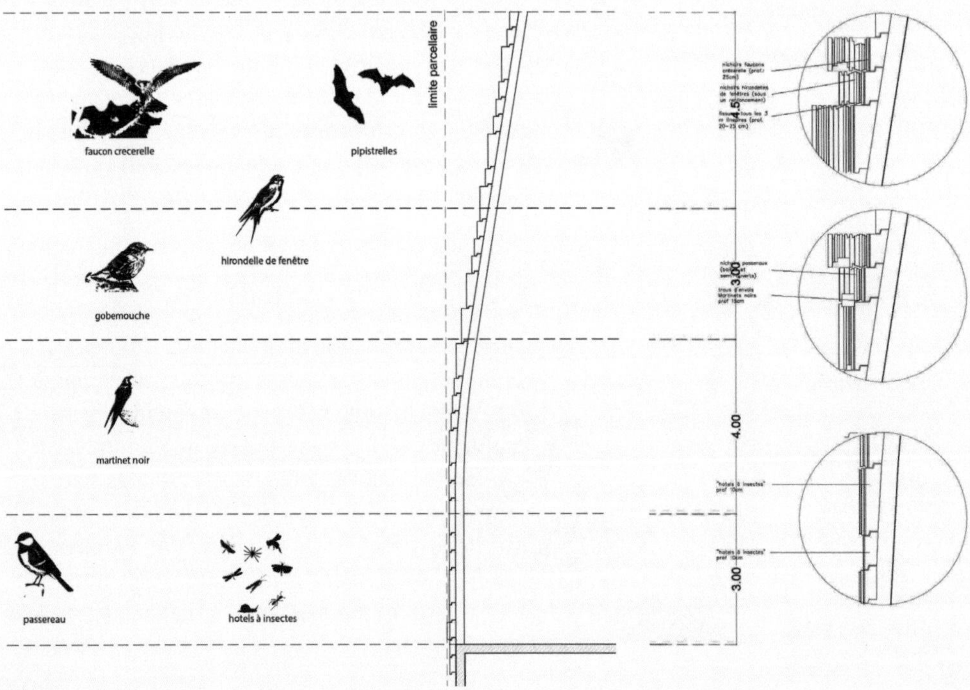

Ridges on top of the concrete outer shell of the facade collect substrate on which mosses or, in this case, windblown sedum can establish itself / The decision has been made to plant in the open ground around the building / The surface area of the prefab facade elements has been increased by creating holes of three to ten millimeters in the end walls.

Outdoor playground / Volunteers, architects from ChartierDelix and ecologists together mow the meadows of the Estate of Marly to then re-sow the roof of the Ecole des sciences et de la biodiversité with the seeds thus collected.

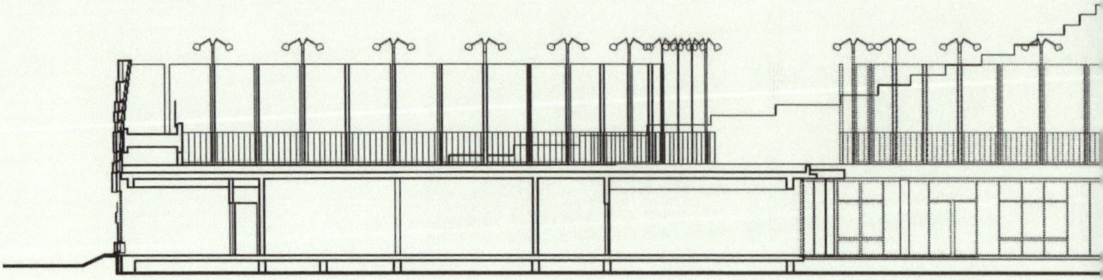

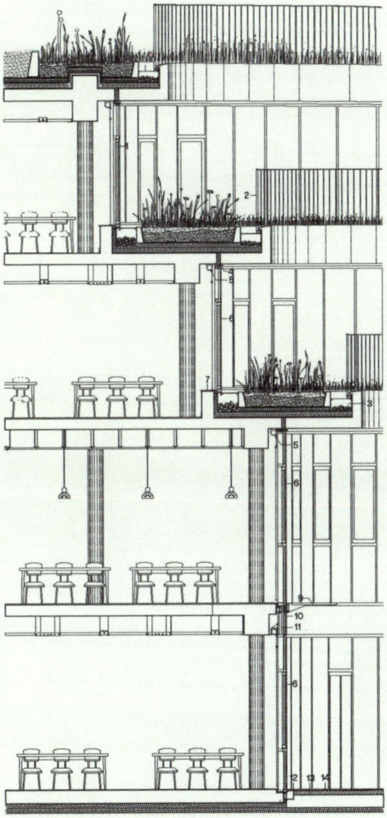

The classrooms offer a view of the green terraces.

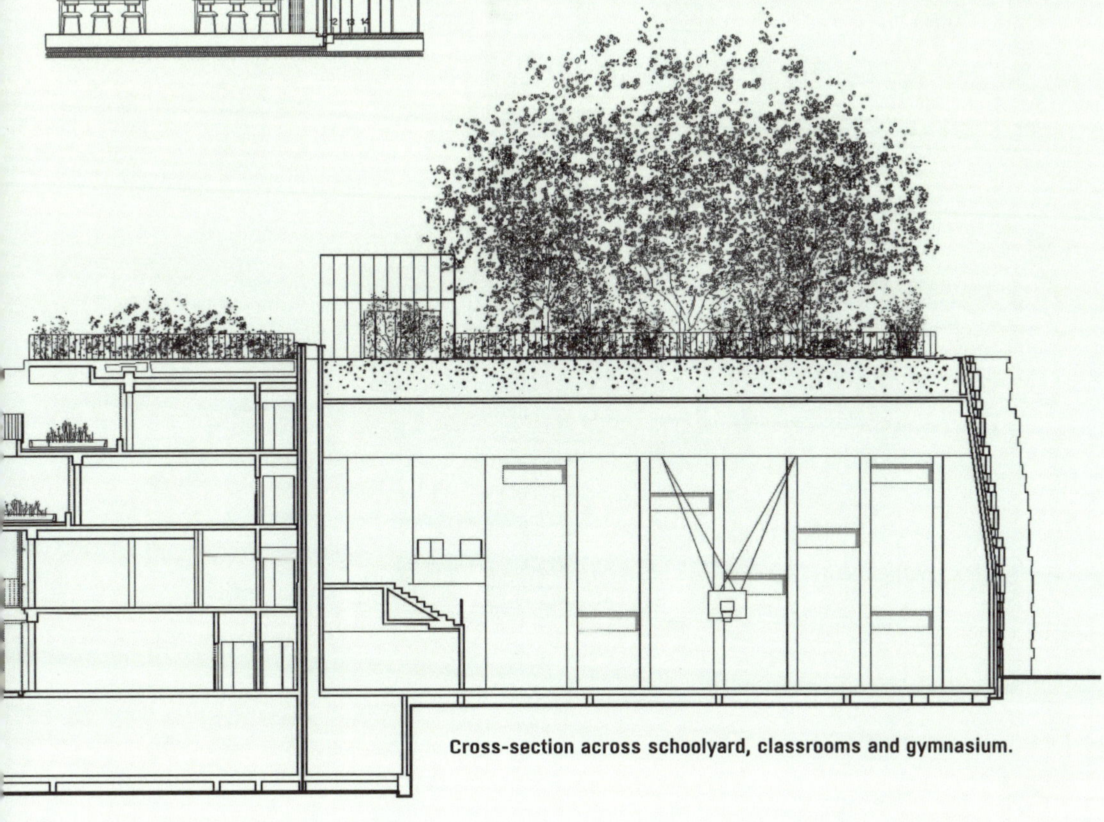

Cross-section across schoolyard, classrooms and gymnasium.

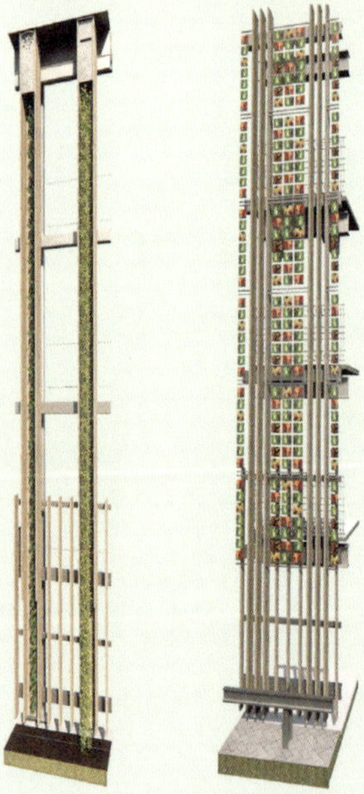

2,1m
15

Demountable car park

Delft, wUrck architectuur stedenbouw landschap, 2022, NL

The wooden facade of this demountable car park on the TU Delft campus has been designed to allow various types of climbing and creeping plants to grow against it. A mix of plant species was chosen so that the flowering season lasts longer and insects can find nectar over a longer period. Moreover, the building has a nice appearance throughout much of the year. At the wooden cassettes are bird and bat boxes and insect hotels. The slats of the cassettes provide additional shelter for birds and bats. The position of the nest boxes is determined according to the sun and wind load and varies per facade. A green fringe (herb roof) is created around the roof edge, contributing to water storage on the roof and to the cooling of the building.

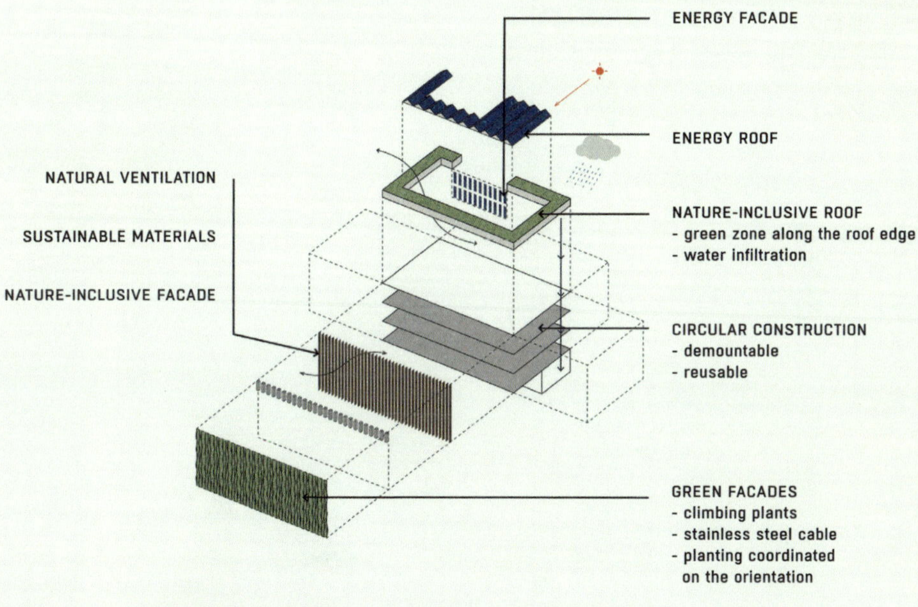

Above: Structure of the car park.
Left: South-west facade / Insects, bats and birds nest boxes on the edges of the roof / Detail of wooden cassettes with tension cables and planting / Green and energy facade elements / Entrance of car park / Roof edge with nest boxes.

4

Everything man is doing in architecture is to try to go against nature. Of course we have to understand nature to know how far we have to go against nature. The secret, I think, of the future is not doing too much. All architects have the tendency to do too much.

FREI OTTO

Building, Flora & Fauna

Numerous plants and animals use buildings as (part of) their habitat. There are many factors that influence their presence. In ecology, a distinction is made between biotic and abiotic factors. Biotic factors concern life itself: the plants, animals and organisms, including their secretions and their behaviour (such as predation). Abiotic factors concern the non-living parts of a biotope that enable and influence the presence of life, such as climate, and the type and chemical composition of the soil.

Abiotic

On average, cities have a higher temperature than the surrounding land and that's why they are sometimes called 'heat islands'. This gives many species of plants and animals an advantage. But if, for example due to the lack of shade in densely built-up city districts, the temperature rises locally and heat stress develops, it can also turn into a disadvantage. This in turn can lead to accelerated parching. With taller buildings, wind can be an additional cause of dry conditions.

Large parts of the surface in cities are paved, and as a result there is a water shortage on the one hand and a water surplus on the other. The shortage can occur because the soil cannot retain the water due to insufficient infiltration through the paved surface (paving and buildings) or because it is drained too quickly in order to avoid any inconveniences. The surplus is caused by the peaks in rainfall, where the paving causes water to stagnate and accumulate locally for a short period of time resulting in nuisance, especially for people. In general, however, cities are typically dry.

Urban soils are often disturbed by the frequent construction, excavation and backfilling of soil and sand. This can make the composition of the soil very diverse and also introduce compositions and seeds foreign to the area.

In cities, the air is of poorer quality on average. This can have a negative effect on species, or favour a selection of species that can cope with it. In addition, the city is a tremendous source of light pollution. Artificial light often has a negative effect on the circadian rhythms of animals (and people), especially on nocturnal species such

Place Charles de Gaulle, Paris.

Food, Security and Reproduction of the mason bee.

as bats and migratory birds. Sound in the form of noise (volume higher than normal everyday acoustics) can be disruptive and stress-inducing for birds in particular. The city also produces excessive amounts of sound, which can disrupt communication between species or their territorial behaviour. Birds may leave the nest, thereby adversely affecting or losing a brood. The city is particularly home to species that have a tolerance to these factors, but also for these there is a limit to what they can handle.

Biotic

Many biotic factors collectively determine the health of an ecosystem. These include the interaction between species, such as symbiosis or competition, the continuation or disruption of the nutrient cycle, genetic variation within a species, and so on. By no means can all these factors be meaningfully influenced by the way the city is built or designed. To nonetheless get some grip on the settlement factors that can be influenced by building or planting, five rules of thumb are often used. These conditions for settlement are: Food (including water), Safety (including places to find shelter and to rest), Reproduction (including places to nest and opportunities to find a mate), Connection and Variety. There are positive and negative approaches to these five conditions: remove one of them and a species will find it harder or even impossible to survive. Promote one of them and biodiversity may benefit. They are five 'knobs to turn'. The red mason bee may serve as an example to illustrate all five conditions. This wild bee, commonly found in urban areas, finds nectar (food) in various flowering plants (variety), shelter (safety) in the greenery of nearby gardens and parks (connection) and builds its nest (reproduction) in cracks and crannies in buildings, trees and in bee hotels placed by human residents.

Food and Water

A primary condition for settlement is the presence of food. And there is food to be found in the city. For many species, in fact, there is plenty of food. Some animals therefore fare better in urban areas than in the countryside. Some animals are attracted to litter (so that is also a way to keep many species in check: don't leave food scraps on the streets). Many species find fruits, berries or nectar in urban gardens and parks, for example. Other species such as predators hunt prey animals present in the city. Plants get their food from the soil and to a small extent from the air. Together with sunlight and water, the presence of soil nutrients is a primary condition for flora to take hold in cities. For both plants and animals, food includes water as a prerequisite for life, although there are species that take in moisture mainly by eating prey animals.

The long-eared owl finds shelter in the dense greenery of an allotment garden.

Safety, Including Shelter and Rest

The fact that there are animals in the city is a sign that the city is safe enough at least for those species. Species to which this does not apply will leave. And vice versa: species that are hunted in the countryside have sometimes moved into the city, such as the fox (which of course also, or firstly, comes to the city for food). There are green areas in the city where it is quiet and dark in the evening, and therefore safe for many species. Examples of extra quiet and therefore safe places include cemeteries and allotment gardens. Trees, shrubs and hedges are of great importance for sheltering birds and small mammals, which is precisely why these species are not found everywhere in the city: a layer for safety, shelter and rest is missing in certain areas. And these animals need to be protected from enemies and weather conditions.

As for plants, they need to be 'safe' from pesticides, mowing, weeding and too much disturbance from human use. Plants should be given time to set seed before they disappear or are removed.

Reproduction, Including Nesting Places and Opportunities to Find a Mate

Reproduction is one of the hallmarks of life, a prerequisite for the survival of the species. Animals need to be able to find a mate and make or find a nest or other place of similar function for the young. Females and males must be able to come into contact with each other so that eggs can be fertilized, whether after mating or not, and then there has to be a safe place for the young to grow up. Where partners cannot interact and/or where nesting opportunities are lacking, the species will leave and look for other opportunities within or outside the city.

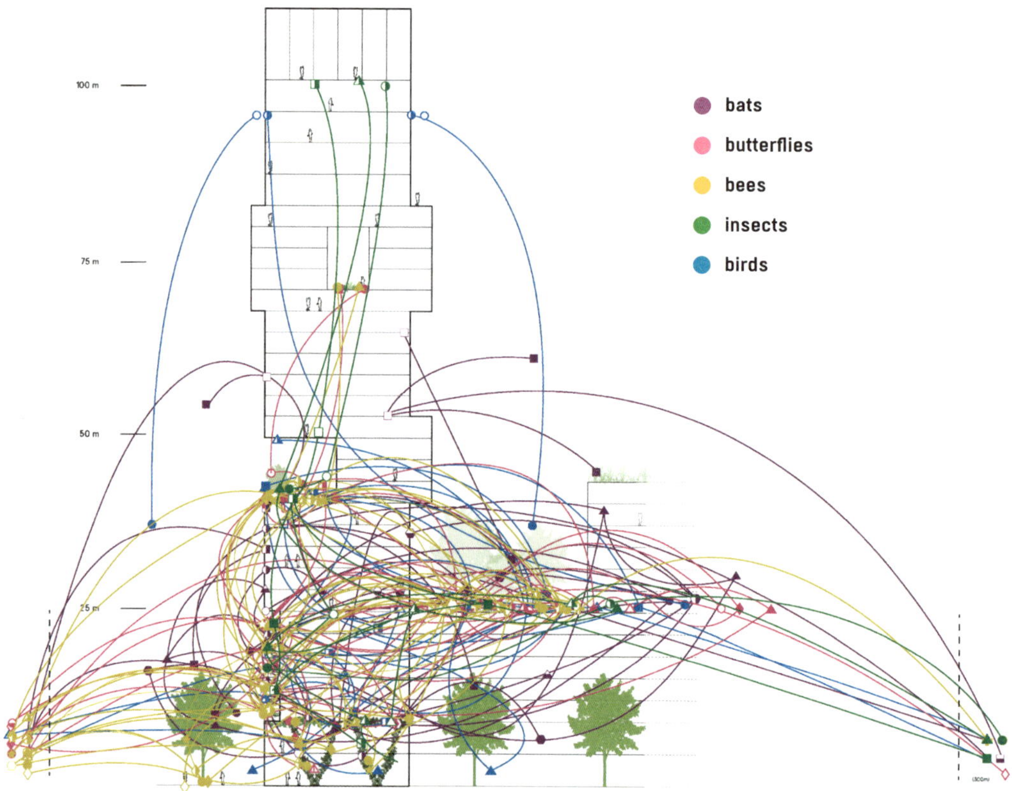

Map of possible relationships of birds, insects and bats with future high-rise buildings. (Trekvlietzone, Flux Landscape Architecture, 2018, NL)

Some plants pollinate themselves or have asexual reproduction through, for example, root shoots or tubers (whereby they clone themselves). But most plants depend on external pollination. This can take place through wind and water, or with the help of pollinating organisms such as insects, or by birds and mammals spreading fruits and seeds.

Connection

A major problem for urban animals and plants is the fragmentation and isolation of areas. For animals, there have to be connections between the foraging area and the nesting site, between resting places and mating places, and so on. These connections are of great importance in a habitat. They are often parallel to those of human infrastructure, by the way; verges along connecting roads, waterways with vegetated quays and banks and such. At the same time, human connections can equally constitute barriers for species, or become the sites of traffic casualties because the different connections are at right angles to each other.

For plants, isolation is also a problem. A population can become too small and thus vulnerable to fluctuations that cannot be absorbed, and isolated areas can cause genetic impoverishment. When areas are connected, plants can move along with changing climatic conditions, and insects can more easily find the plants for pollination.

Higher up, a green roof functions as a stepping stone in the green urban web / Adding green to facades brings variation and provides connections from the street level to the roof.

For both plants and animals, a connection can sometimes also function if there are so-called stepping stones: small areas that enable exchange because they are a short distance from each other, ultimately connecting two larger areas.

Variation

For animals and plants, variation (diversity) is very important. On the one hand, variation of living conditions in the environment creates more opportunities for the settling of different animals and plants. Think of variation in sun/shade, wet/dry, high/low, nutrient-poor/rich, wind/lee or soil type. Each species has its own preference and range (minimum-optimum-maximum) so can occupy its own niche. Furthermore, variation provides more resilience when conditions change. For instance, if it gets drier, but there is a gradient from wet to dry, a plant or animal can move on.

On the other hand, variation within the totality of different species is also important. Many different flowering plants mean that there is a long 'bloom period' and insects can forage for as long as possible, or that many different animals can eat plants.

And finally, variation is important for the urban ecosystem as a whole. More interactions can occur when there is a greater variety of areas and species. This can lead to complex food webs and symbiotic relationships, where different species depend on but can also benefit from each other.

Urban Flora and Fauna

Besides insects, birds and bats, other mammals, amphibians and reptiles are also found on buildings. Fish, molluscs and a variety of macrofauna also live in urban water. As these species are only found to a limited extent on buildings, they will not be described separately, but where applicable in the project descriptions. These will also include our pets, most notably the domestic cat. Nature-exclusive building deals with species for which we as humans do *not* want to make provisions, whether deliberate or unintentional.

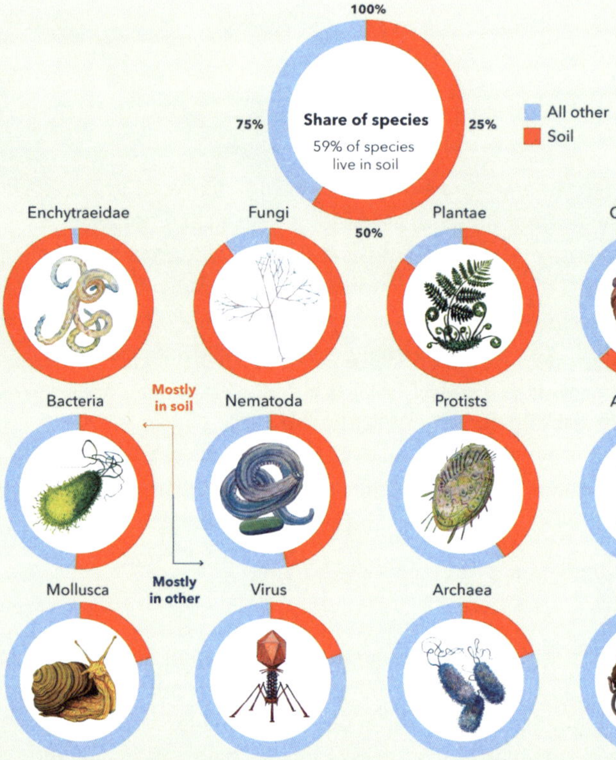

Charles Darwin described earthworms as 'nature's workers' and estimated that every so many years the complete surface layer of the world would pass the stomachs of earthworms. Earthworms play such a big role in the soil's ecology mainly because the species is so incredibly numerous. It is estimated that earthworms make up roughly half of the soil's biomass.

Soil Life

Beneath our feet, there is an entire ecosystem of organisms whose main task together is to break down waste from the food pyramid; the so-called decomposers. They convert organic manure, dead animals and plant residues into nutrients. In doing so, they provide raw materials that are essential for the growth of plants, which are primary producers in ecosystems. In addition, soil life ensures good soil structure by loosening the soil, mixing organic and inorganic matter and limiting pathogens. In agricultural areas, soil life also provides (partly, if the quantities are not too large) nitrogen fixation. Many soil fungi form a mutualistic symbiosis with other plants, where there is mutual benefit in obtaining nutrients. It has also recently been discovered that plants and trees can communicate with each other through elaborate systems of fungi, forming superorganisms.

Soil life is thus a crucial link in the cycle of life, but these functions and their associated organisms have hardly been properly mapped. In cities, and certainly under and near buildings, the soil has been made virtually sterile by construction projects and fill sand, and trees and plants in these places already experience acute stress because of the lack of these nutrients and associated soil life. These therefore often have to be replenished artificially.

It is very important for further development of a more natural city and building to increase the knowledge of soil life in these 'underdeveloped areas', in order to then be able to take measures that will eventually lead to soil improvement in the city. This is not yet the case, although there has been more attention for it recently. For now, the main issue is to preserve the soil life present on the construction site and not to unnecessarily remove soil and replace it with a 'dead' sand package.

The interaction between these soil species within a food web is as complex and the species richness is as diverse as that of above-ground ecosystems. Organisms present in the (healthy) soil include: bacteria and actinomycetes (filamentous bacteria), fungi, protozoa (unicellular organisms), nematodes, springtails, mites, potworms (small worms, but not earthworms), centipedes, insects, spiders, earthworms and moles and others.

The total biomass of the most common organisms in relation to the total biomass of humans.

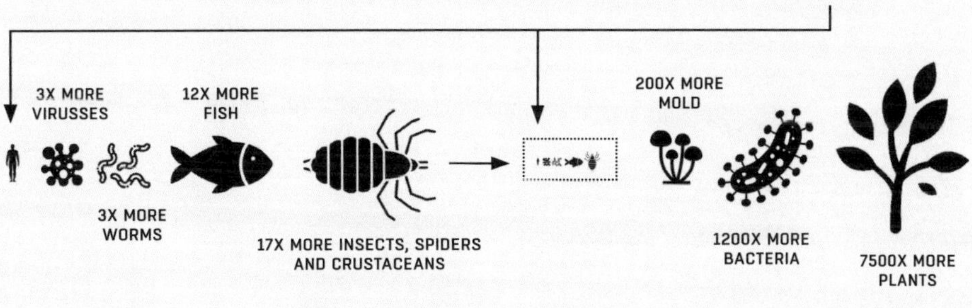

Building & Flora

Plants are at the basis of life. They are an essential link in the cycle of life because plants, like algae and some bacteria, convert energy from sunlight into glucose through photosynthesis. In the process, they assimilate carbon dioxide from the atmosphere and produce oxygen. In addition, they absorb certain essential nutrients from the soil and pass them on to species higher up the food chain.

Without plants, there can be no biodiversity: they provide habitats and food sources for countless animals, including insects, birds and mammals. Plants are therefore sometimes referred to as the backbone of the ecosystem. In cities, plants also provide a number of important services to people and animals: they improve air quality and reduce the heat island effect, on the one hand through evaporation and on the other through shade, and their CO2-assimilation helps mitigate the damage caused by the climate crisis. So we cannot exist without plants.

Flora can be divided into seed plants (flowering plants and gymnosperms), spore plants (including ferns, horsetails and ground pines), mosses and algae. Lichens are a symbiosis of an alga with a fungus. Seed plants generally receive the most attention, because of the blooms and seeds that are essential food for many species, but certainly also because people appreciate them for their looks, colour and smell. Spore plants, such as ferns and some mosses, including several rare, spontaneously occurring species, usually thrive in shaded and moist environments in a garden or on (quay) walls. Quay walls in particular can produce rich wall vegetation. Mosses receive much less attention, not to mention algae and lichens. Yet each of these life forms has its own role in the ecosystem and can have a place on or be attached to the building. How rich this can turn out to be can be seen at facade walls with leaking gutters or rain spots. What happened here by accident can be a nice inspiration for nature-inclusive buildings, letting rainwater deliberately drain via facade walls.

About two-thirds of the Dutch flora is found to a greater or lesser extent in urban areas and slightly less than half, the true urban plants (city-dependent and city-loving species), are really at home in the city. But not in every city. The flora of cities is quite similar, but each city also has its own peculiarities; specific species that are often related to a city's location (geographical regions) and (historical) urban spatial structure.

At the same time, a trend can be observed in north-western Europe that, due to similar design and materialization of public spaces, and the equal degree of densification, cities are becoming more and more alike: so-called biodiversity flattening. Special niches are

A screen of different types of facade vegetation, (Stadthaus M1, Barkow+Leibinger, 2013).

disappearing, in particular the 'rough city' with its unused spots and still undesignated vacant lots and associated unique species.
At the same time, the assortment sold through garden centres in particular introduces new species, which then spread in the urban environment. This concerns not only the plants themselves; even with imported tub plants (especially olive trees and fan palms), non-native species can inadvertently come along from faraway places and establish themselves in cities. Through global commodity trade, seeds also come into our cities in other ways with all kinds of products. In addition, many species from other countries are intentionally planted because of their ornamental value in public outdoor spaces or because non-native trees have qualities that are desirable, such as their ability to cope with air pollution, root pressure and heat. This introduction of new species has been going on since the Middle Ages, including now highly valued favourites such as ivy-leaved toadflax and wallflower. More than half of today's urban plants are of foreign origin: partly from (nearby) European regions, but equally from other continents. There has long been an established term for these species new to a particular area: neophytes, which translates as 'newcomers'. Nowadays, they are increasingly presented as exotics, often with a negative connotation, mainly associated with a small group of invasive species. However, research shows that more than 95 per cent of newcomers fit in with our flora, taking up mostly unoccupied niches. In doing so, these species can be of value and contribute to an ecosystem, as has already happened with ivy-leaved toadflax, wallflower and yellow corydalis. Climate change is also changing the flora per region: heat causes southern species to move further north. In the process, new species appear, while species that are less resistant to increasing heat and drought disappear.

In general, native plants strengthen the ecosystem the most because they have established unique relationships with insects, birds and other organisms in the area concerned. For example, some species of wild bees and bumblebees depend on a limited number of plant species. Sometimes even just a single species of host plant. Many species of butterflies have only a limited number of plants on which they lay eggs. And various insects' tongues or proboscises, for example, are adapted to certain types of plants or have developed a technique tailored to the plant. Some plants in turn have adapted to the insects to ensure that they are pollinated: the process of so-called co-evolution. The plant-animal relationship is therefore very specific for specialized species. New in this regard is the insight that the designation 'native species' needs a critical revision, where the addition of autochthonous origin (plant from the area) is essential. By now, it has become clear that for native species, it matters what their area of origin is; the wild pedunculate oak in Spain is different (genetically and in ecological relationships) from that in our northern regions. The same applies to many wild plants that we sow as native; they often look different too. With that sowing, existing populations with unique characteristics are at risk of disappearing. Hence, there is a new focus on working with local material (seeds).

Environmental Factors

The city is not the friendliest environment for many plants. Besides relatively more drought and heat, there is much more stone, root pressure and compaction, weed

City walls and quay walls form an ideal biotope for species such as the ivy-leaved toadflax and yellow corydalis.

control and the use of road salt. At the same time, these dynamics also provide opportunities for species that can tolerate this or even prefer it. Think of the real cosmopolitans, the plants that can be found in every street and feel perfectly at home there. And the city is not exactly a homogeneous area: in addition to places with a lot of human influence and intensive use, there are also very quiet forgotten spots in a city, such as sloping banks along infrastructure, derelict corners where no building takes place for a while, or grassy patches on the edges of the city or along infrastructure where few people come. The city has many biotopes.

That the city is a serious subject of study for botanists is evidenced by the fact that the urban district has become its own entity in the flora districts of the Netherlands and Flanders. The urban flora has its own characteristics and has sufficient species diversity to arrive at this classification. Characteristics of the urban district include urban soils (stony and disturbed soil layers), different environmental conditions and a warmer urban climate.

Many animal species also make use of the spontaneous flora that are usually labelled as 'weeds'. These include knotgrass, annual meadow grass, lamb's quarters, mugwort, dandelion, plantain, shepherd's purse and nettle. For example, nettle is the host plant of the red admiral and other butterflies, and dandelion provides nectar to bumblebee queens, wild bees and hoverflies in early spring. One of the threats to spontaneous flora in the city is that vacant lots, with characteristic spontaneous vegetation, are increasingly being landscaped, temporarily or otherwise. We often fail to leave a wild patch of urban nature alone and intact. In fact, there is a tendency to sow it (for 'the bees') without recognizing the ecological significance of such an area. But bees benefit from a natural vegetation rich in structure and variety rather than from a verge full of colourful flowers that have just been sown and after a few years turns into a disruptive vegetation.

If the city fails to preserve a piece of vacant land as an urban nature reserve, this could at least be compensated by providing such biotopes on green roofs scattered around the city.

Another threat to spontaneous urban flora is the (frequent) cleaning and restoration of city walls and canals, on which valuable wall flora occurs. When these walls are periodically cleaned, valuable wall vegetation is lost. Walls that are damp and have chalky mortar are in fact an opportunity to use nature-inclusive building to ensure that this biotope remains present in the city. It has now become apparent that an excellent structural condition of a wall is compatible with the preservation of wall vegetation.

On a green roof, variation can be stimulated by relief in the substrate (soil) on the roof. Here, more weight can be placed in the constructive zones and thus a thicker package, creating height differences and thereby diversity in planting.

Some cities now have a policy of applying wall-plant-friendly mortar in all new quay walls. This is a big change from traditional wall management. The motto is no longer to remove vegetation, but to allow and foster it. Only ligneous species should be removed because their roots may eventually push stones apart.
Trees are an important part of urban flora, but they are vulnerable. Trees only live to an average of 30 years in the city, because of frequent redevelopment, the roots not having enough space in the subsoil which limits growth and stability, or due to changes in water levels or damage to the tree by construction work or traffic. Older trees are therefore often found in places where they have space and are left alone; in cemeteries, allotments, in parks and along the scarce old structures in the city that are left undisturbed. Trees are important for all kinds of life in the city: for people, animals and plants. There are plants that only grow on or attached to trees, and all kinds of animal species depend on trees for food, shelter and reproduction.

Water, nutrients, and light are the conditions for the growth of trees and other plants. Most plants get their nutrients directly from the soil, but some plants get their moisture with nutrients from other plants as parasites (on another living plant, harming the host) or saprophytes (on dead material). There are also plants that need another plant as a support, such as epiphytes that grow in trees without affecting the tree, for example common polypody. And finally, there is a system of mutualism, where species have a mutually beneficial cooperation. A good example here is the relationship between mycorrhizal fungi and plants: the fungi, with their extensive branching, efficiently extract nutrients from the soil and supply this to the plant via the roots; the plant, in turn, supplies sugars back to the fungus. Trees are known to depend on mycorrhizal fungi to absorb sufficient nutrients, but this is also true for some orchid species, such as the bee orchid.

An example of a fully-fledged green roof on a car park. Complete with water feature and elevations in the roof landscape. (Left and above: green roof carpark European Patent Office, Rijswijk, Copijn, 1997, NL)

Soil and the soil life it contains form the basis for flora and fauna higher up in the food pyramid. There are big differences in the quality of soils and thus soil life in the city. The nature of the soil ranges from nutrient-poor to very rich (overfertilized), the soil life from poor to moderate. However, thanks to the diversity of soil composition, available nutrients and substrates (including walls and embankments), the diversity of the present flora is relatively high.
Cities are characterized by a relatively dry climate, making water scarce in many parts. The main cause is that it is drained away too quickly via paved surfaces (roads, paths, buildings) and not retained in the soil. In addition, space for plants, and for trees in particular, is often limited. A larger planting bed helps species, because then there is more rooting space, and more unpaved surface generally means more availability of water and nutrients. Another reason for a drier city is that it is warmer (and buildings still radiate heat even at night, especially in summer) and thus there is more evaporation.
In relation to the building, there is no such thing as a natural soil. A soil on a green roof is of a very different order from that at ground level, where there is also contact with groundwater. It is worth bearing in mind that erecting a building comes at the expense of soil life and thus the other species that use it. A green roof does not compensate for this. This is why it is very important that in construction work the soil is left intact as much as possible during the work and is not routinely excavated and loaded with a thick layer of sand when there is no need for this.
Water on a roof can be collected in a system under the substrate, but also partly in the substrate layer. Water retention can provide the right conditions for plants. However, it will rarely be fully self-sufficient; in the dry months of the year, most plants without contact with groundwater simply need to be watered. Only species that are extremely drought-resistant, such as many species of mosses and sedums, do survive for long

A row of mature pedunculate oaks was spared and integrated into the design. The canopy provides shade in summer. (Care residences De Eiken, Zoersel, Monnikenheide, UR architects, 2020, B)

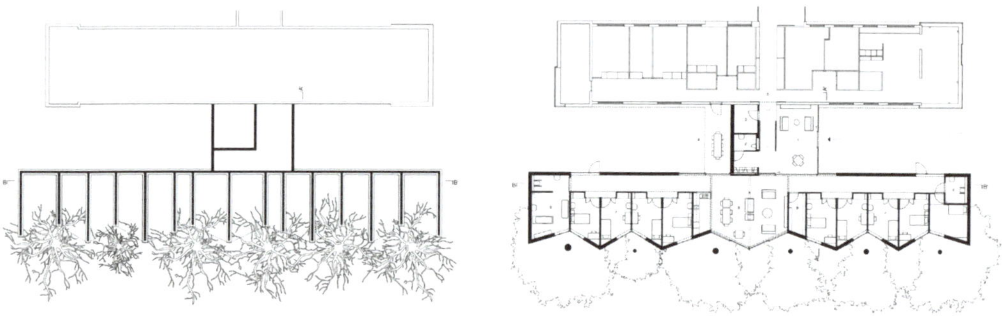

To construct the building at a short distance from the trees without damaging the roots, a comb-shaped foundation was chosen / The construction of the bicycle shed also spared the trees.

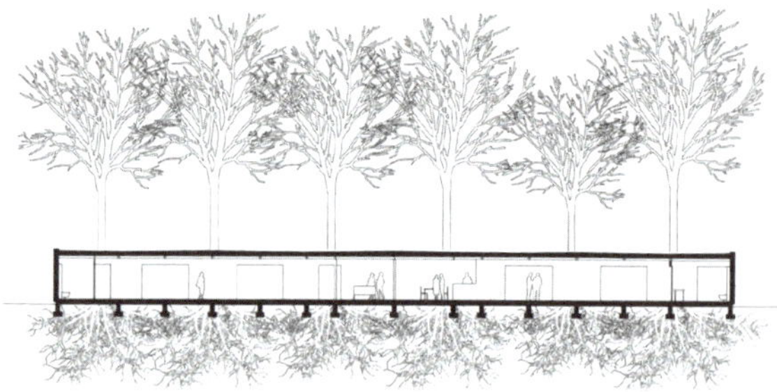

periods without water. An additional dimension can be added to these green roofs by focusing on more naturally sparse, drought-resistant vegetation, such as dune roofs. The biggest threats to urban flora are human interventions. Here, too, management is important. If plants are cut before flowering and seed setting, they will eventually disappear. Pruning too often or too far back can cause problems for a shrub or tree. Match the layout and management to the desired plant species and specify long-term management and maintenance in a management plan. Adjust the layout based on monitoring. Especially for green roofs, this is an important part of the sustainable maintenance of plants on a roof.

A building can be a link in a connection for plant species. Especially if this building thereby contributes to a green structure in a stony part of the city. Green roofs and facades will function as new links in the network (as stepping stones). Besides planting, a roof can also host spontaneous vegetation, which generally will come with the wind. Conversely, the roof can be used as a source of seed for the environment. The seeds of preferably native plants can thus blow or fall down over the city. As a huge seed bomb, Édouard François used the roof garden of his 60-metre tower in Paris to select native plants whose seeds can spread across the city.

The transition between the ground level and the building is a crucial element in the design and allows species to reach the building from a short distance.

Species Groups

A healthy ecosystem benefits from variation created by achieving different biotic and abiotic conditions. One way to create more variety with greenery is stratification. In the city, the layer between one to six metres in height, the space between grass vegetation and tree crown, is often missing. This is the place where shrubs and smaller ligneous species (in technical terms: third-sized trees, which can reach a height of eight metres at most) can be found and which many animal species make grateful use of for shelter, foraging and nesting. It is therefore important that there is variation in the height of greenery to promote biodiversity. Such diversity is especially high in so-called mantle and fringe vegetation: where the planting curves down from trees via lower trees (such as blackthorn, rowan), shrubs (hazel, honeysuckle, traveller's joy, wild privet, bramble and elder), to herbs (such as greater yellow rattle, nettle, yarrow, sorrel, trefoil, dandelion).

Trees

The combination of buildings and trees is an age-old theme in architecture. Planted when the structure was erected or spared out of respect for the tree's beauty and history, there are examples of buildings that go hand in hand with 'their' tree for often centuries-old reasons. Alternatively, existing, monumental groups of trees can inspire a special design. The insight that trees play an important role in the ecosystem and provide shade and clean urban air has made the regular felling of trees during construction a thing of the past. Better still, tree planting has become part of the climate-adaptive urban plan. To determine the number of trees in a design, the 3-30-300 rule was introduced.

Bosco Verticale is the most high-profile example of a building where mature trees are part of the architecture. This trend is driven by ecosystem services such as the

The 3-30-300 rule states that everyone should be able to see at least 3 trees from their home, every neighbourhood should have 30 per cent tree canopy coverage and high-quality green public space should be available within 300 metres. (source: Cecil Konijnendijk, NBSI)

shading and cooling that trees provide and the aspiration to increase urban biodiversity. However, planting trees on buildings has its limitations. Trees are highly dependent on the artificial supply of nutrients and irrigation due to the limited soil depth. Also, maintenance at this height is important and complex because falling branches can cause damage. Special attention should be paid to the anchoring of trees. At higher altitudes, wind loads are greater and, combined with a smaller soil mass, trees should therefore be braced to prevent them from toppling over.
It is always wise to give a green structure time to develop. Through succession, tree saplings can become part of the ecosystem on facades and roofs. Possible trees on a roof are Japanese flowering crabapple, hazel, serviceberry and rowan. Species tolerant to drought and wind are also often sought, such as cottoneaster and tamarisk. In the M6B2 project, a residential tower in Paris, small oaks growing in narrow tubes were chosen. This takes time, but the chances of survival are better in the longer term.

Shrubs

Shrubs have woody branches just like trees, but unlike a tree, which has a single trunk, shrubs branch directly at the ground. They are also generally a bit smaller and more compact than trees, which makes them a little easier to use on, for example, green roofs. Incidentally, some shrubs, such as the serviceberry, can be grown in a tree form. Soil and moisture are also essential for shrubs. This is easier to achieve in open ground than in a roof pack of limited depth. Shrubs such as common barberry, bush ivy, blackcurrant, dog-rose, redcurrant, sweet briar, raspberry, elder, wild privet, firethorn and laurel are suitable not only as a food source, but also as a shelter and nesting place for birds.

As a rule, shrubs do better on a green roof than trees because of the rooting space and moisture supply. Some shrubs can grow up to 'tree-like' size. Again, the thicker the soil pack, the more options are available and the better the shrubs can do given the constraints in terms of heat, wind and moisture.

Climbing Plants
Facade landscaping has a long history. As part of the landscaping of estates and castles, it also made its appearance in more urban structures in the late nineteenth century. There are many types of climbing plants, subdivided into self-attachers, creepers and vines. The best-known climber is ivy, which is naturally a forest plant that grows well in the shade. Ivy flowers in autumn, for which it must be at least ten years old and not over-pruned during that period, but then it is one of the last flowering plants of the year and important for bees. It is a plant that attaches itself directly to the surface, its roots seeking hold in cracks and crannies. The ivy is listed as a native plant unlike the wisteria, which has been introduced. Wisteria blooms profusely in spring, and the nectar from the flower clusters attracts numerous solitary bees, bumblebees and butterflies. This woody creeper can grow up to 20 metres tall and needs a sturdy climbing support to do so. This also applies to traveller's joy, which is native and has properties similar to wisteria.
The mile-a-minute vine is a plant that is also common as a facade climber. Originating from Asia, this plant grows from the open ground via vines up the facade. As a flowering plant, it is attractive to insects, and birds can hide in it.

Wall plants
Wall plants are bound to soft, calcareous mortars that are still standard in traditional masonry in listed buildings. Apart from these, they have fallen into disuse. With the advent of modern hard mortars, many wall plants suffered, but locally, beautiful wall vegetation has still developed. The significance of this is now more widely recognized, with all kinds of project initiatives using 'old-fashioned' mortar with all kinds of additional benefits. There are also more options to literally give wall plants space too. In a design, small spaces can be saved for ivy-leaved toadflax and maidenhair spleenwort, for example. Sedum species such as biting stonecrop (whether introduced from the roof or not) can grow on a concrete surface or in a joint with little substrate.

Sedums
There are several species of sedum, originally rock-dwelling succulents, with in our area (north-western Europe) also native species such as biting stonecrop, white stonecrop and reflexed stonecrop that flourish on sandy, stony (rocky) soils in our urban areas, on railway and factory sites, and on quays and walls. While the plant was first frequently grown as a garden plant due to its low maintenance requirements, it is now becoming widespread due to its application on roofs with a thin substrate layer. On green roofs, a mix of sedum species is often used including species from southern, mountainous areas (such as Spanish stonecrop), which can withstand the heat and drought on urban roofs well.

Grasses, sedum and herb vegetation on a green roof.

Low-tech: A continuous groove was inserted at the front of this sitting stairs. Rainwater running over the stairs moistens the brick substructure. In combination with the high air humidity of the pond at the base of the stairs the ideal conditions are created for hart's-tongue ferns and other wall plants. (Overgrown sitting stairs, campus TU Delft, 2018, NL) / Hart's tongue in the shadow against a damp wall.

Water is prerequisite for mosses to grow in a shady environment.

Herbs and Grasses
Vegetation rich in herbs provides nectar, seeds and small fruits for insects and birds. When choosing herbs, there is a distinction between annuals, biennials and perennials. When planting, perennials are preferable, annuals and biennials can also appear spontaneously or be sown to a limited extent if desired for the overall look. It is not possible to give a list of ideal plants, as this strongly depends on the conditions and, for biodiversity, a diversity of plants should be sought above all. However, to give some examples, think of common yarrow, chives, harebell, wild marjoram, vervain, tasteless stonecrop, meadow clary, lesser calamint, bladder campion, primrose and maiden pink. Preferably use native species with seeds from your own local area. Note that grass is dominant, so do not sow that with the seeds.
Grasses with seeds are good for all kinds of birds, and these often occur spontaneously on green roofs. Planted grasses are often the ornamental grasses with little value for biodiversity. However, these are resistant to drought and heat and are of particular visual value to people. Grasses also come in many varieties with, on roofs, ornamental grasses such as silky spice melic, feathergrass in addition to natural components: drooping brome, junegrass and wood small-reed.

Ferns and Mosses
Ferns and mosses are found in humid and shady places such as around bridges and quays and other urban infrastructural structures. Wall-rue and hart's-tongue fern can occur in these places if they are calcareous enough. Rarer, more critical species such as brittle bladder fern, black spleenwort and rustyback can also occur when the conditions are right.
Mosses can grow in almost all places, from nutrient-rich soil to poor sand and from a stone wall to even plastic material, such as a garden table. Many species can also survive in extreme conditions on roofs and walls of buildings, in both very dry and sunny and very wet conditions. And in the city, species such as wall screw moss can also cope well with moderate air quality. Usually, providing a variety of substrates and refraining from cleaning is enough to get mosses to grow on buildings.

Lichens
Lichens attach themselves to the stones of walls and pavements. In more porous material, lichens can find a place to grow. Lichens grow particularly well in areas with low air pollution, clean air and sufficient humidity. This can be managed by creating shaded areas on a wall and by ensuring that walls are not cleaned, as lichens do not grow quickly. Lichens are eaten by snails and some beetles, and in turn provide a habitat for small spiders and small insects such as mites and the caterpillars of some moths.

Biotope City

Wienerberg, IBA, Wenen, various architects, 2013-2021, AT

Biotope City is a densely built-up, green residential area in Vienna. The project was developed on the basis of Helga Fassbinder's 'biotope city' concept. This design principle assumes that increasing liveability and improving biodiversity can go hand in hand in the compact city.

A characteristic feature is the green, car-free outdoor space with herb-rich meadows, open water and large trees. Rainwater is absorbed by the soil, plants and trees. Excess water is stored in a pond at peak loads. The buildings also feature native planting in the form of facade vegetation and green roofs. The buildings are equipped with nesting facilities for birds and bats. Special measures have been taken for eight native species of bats on the buildings and in the greenery around them.

The site covers 5.4 hectares and was previously a fully paved business park. Some of the demolished buildings have been recycled for new construction. The soil, which had been completely covered for decades, has been replenished with 20,000 m^3 of excess 'living' soil from the adjacent Wildgarten new development project. This gives the vegetation a soil similar to that of the surrounding area. The result is a basis for a biotope consisting of native vegetation, local insects and birds that thrive there.

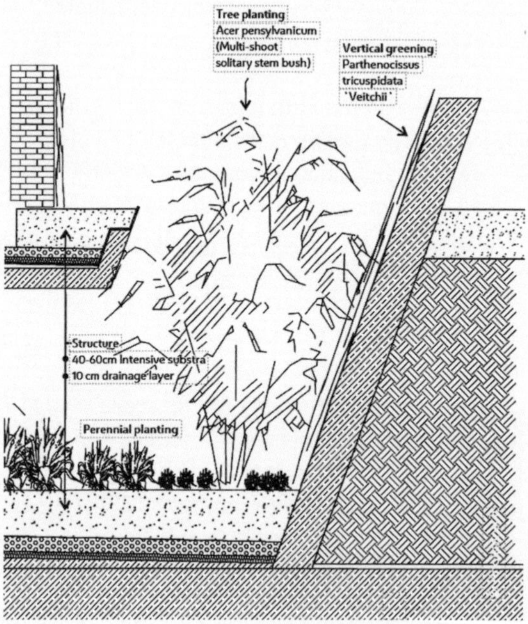

The car parks are located under the residential buildings and are naturally ventilated through vegetated shafts. The plants in these shafts include striped maple and vine.

Left: Cross-section ventilation shaft of the car park / Right: Verges of paths rich with herbs / Pergola with solar panels / Rainwater storage in central pond / Native planting /Plan of Biotope City / Overgrown ventilation shaft of car park.

Het Zandkasteel, Amsterdam

Alberts & Van Huut, Copijn, 1986 / Transformation: Arcadis, Timo Cents, 2023, NL

The building was realized in the 1980s as the headquarters of the NMB bank. The then managing director and client supported the anthroposophical philosophy of life. Based on the ideas of Rudolf Steiner, the building was designed in an organic architectural language with the characteristic oblique corners and a 'natural' colour palette. Due to the colour of the brickwork and the upwardly receding facades, it was popularly nicknamed 'the Sandcastle'. The building features roof gardens above the car park with a soil package averaging 80 centimetres in which large trees have been able to grow over time. Constructed without a water retention layer and without artificial irrigation this all worked fine for a long time. However, during the hot summers of the past few years extra irrigation proved necessary after all.

Substantial trees now also grow on the terraces on the outside. A special element of the roof landscape are the roof ponds (including waterfall), creating a rich biotope for water-loving insects and thus birds. A sparrow colony has established itself in the roof garden.

Above: The redevelopment plan for the rooftop gardens as part of the transformation into a residential complex with a school.
Left: Birch trees in rooftop garden / Water sculpture / Het Zandkasteel, with trees on the exterior balconies of the building / A now more than 40 years old field maple in the atrium / Roof pond, as present in the original design.

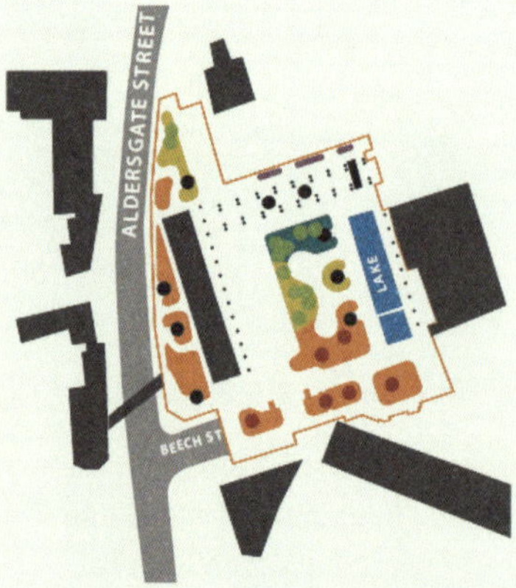

Planting zones, related to sun and shade.

The Barbican

London, Nigel Dunnett, 2015, GB

The Barbican is a brutalist project from the 1970s in London, with large-scale housing developments and the largest centre for culture, arts and conferences in Europe. The traffic infrastructure (park car) is underneath the complex with rooftop gardens and landscaped podium gardens on top of it.

The designer was tasked with making the area drought-proof without using an automated irrigation system. In the context of climate change, technical water systems are no longer considered sustainable, especially if drinking water is used for this purpose. This required radical adaptations. The trees had to be removed in order to replace the waterproof layer underneath the roof garden. The designers involved the residents in the new design. Residents felt attached to the trees, particularly because of the birds. There was also concern about a possible loss of colour and a drab appearance in winter. The result is 'naturalistic' rather than the ordered garden it originally was.

Choosing plants with different flowering periods is not only better for feeding insects. The gardens also have a colourful look throughout the year. By extending the flowering season, nectar is available over a longer period. The insects that benefit from this, in turn, are food for birds and bats. The urban landscape plan is based on a steppe-grass landscape, making an irrigation system unnecessary. Meanwhile, despite the lost trees, breeding birds have been observed again. The shrubs provide ample shelter and nesting opportunities. The planting scheme consists of three plant communities, each designed for different microclimates, with the level of direct sunlight being the determining factor. By combining plants that fit together ecologically, these plant communities together form an ecosystem.

Steppe planting is a mixture of grasses and perennials that are naturally adapted to dry, exposed conditions. This is the main plant type across the site. Very colourful and with diverse foliage textures and plant shapes. Shrub steppe plantings combine perennials and grasses with open shrubs and multi-stemmed trees to create multi-layer plantings with an open structure year-round. Light woodland plantings in part-shade and applied where the substrate depth enables tree growth. Multi-stem trees, widely spaced create a light, open canopy, with a scattered undergrowth of shrubs, and a diverse perennial ground layer.

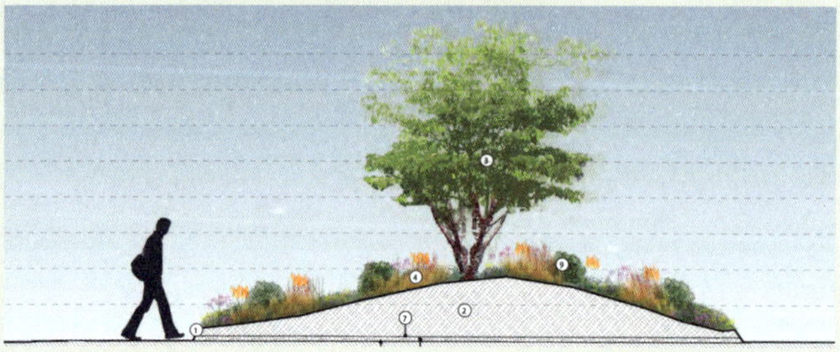

The thickness of the substrate also depends on the loadbearing capacity of the roof of the carpark in different places.

Redesign as a steppe landscape / Steppe planting / Shrub steppe plantings / Light woodland plantings.

Vanishing Staircase

Utrecht, Birthe Leemeijer, Vergroening Singel030, 2018, NL

The stairs start at a window of the Centraal Museum and ends in the water. As a sculpture it makes a connection between the museum and the park, between the park and water, between art and life. The stairs are visited by people, plants and animals, some of whom live there.

By tilting the steps backwards the distinction between high and low is cancelled. Visitors of the park use the Vanishing Staircase to sit there, children run up and down the tilted steps and dogs jump into the water from the lowest step. The bank forms an exit site for aquatic wildlife and is a resting place for ducks.

Residents and ecologists, united in Vergroening Singel030, manage the stairs together. The planting and substrate design is by Paul van Kan and Lies König. The space beside the sculpture and the splits between the steps are planted with native species, which also can be found on the city's wharf walls and the quays of the Stadsbuitengracht. So, plants and their associated fauna also step on the stairs.

Eight ecological zones can be distinguished. There is a gradient from wet to dry, onr from light to shadow and one from slightly acidic to calcareous. At one side of the stairs there is herb-rich meadow land and on the other side we find so-called 'stinzenbulbs' underneath the shrubs and trees.

Left: Residents at work / Tilting the steps allows substrate and water to nurture plant growth in the gaps / Porous stone allow plants to root / Biotope gradient from dry to wet.

Building & Insects

All over the world, insects are receiving more attention than ever, partly because of declining numbers and disappearing species. This is not limited to nature reserves; in the city too, there is justified attention for insect biodiversity. Here, eyes are particularly focused on a number of recognizable groups of pollinators. But specialists also increasingly study all insect life in the city, even finding previously undescribed species, for instance during a so-called bioblitz or a taxon expedition. Insects play a crucial role in every ecosystem, and the built environment can contribute to their habitat.

There are all kinds of insects that like to use a building because of its lee and warmth, because of the cracks and crannies of a building that can serve as a habitat, and because of the food and the possibilities for reproduction and shelter provided by green roofs and facades of buildings. Whether a building is used by insects has a lot to do with its context. The wind factor has a major effect on the presence of insects on buildings. If no wind protection can be found on a green roof, insects will generally only use it sparingly, however good the design may be with, for example, suitable plants that provide nectar and pollen.

There are many different types of insects that can make use of a building. This depends on a good structural variation in soil, the right types of soils, the type of planting, the height of a green roof, and how much sunshine and shelter from the wind there is on the roof.

Insects react quite quickly to changes. As a species group, this makes them very suitable for monitoring. Improvements and deteriorations of a habitat can therefore be noticed relatively early on. These could be changes in layout, maintenance or, on a much larger scale, climate.

Honey bee on an aster.

Environmental Factors

Insects are mobile species and therefore do not directly rely on connections and corridors in urban areas to move between different habitats, food sources and breeding grounds. The city is a heterogeneous area for these species. Most crucial for insects is the presence of suitable habitat itself. Buildings can play a role here by providing a green roof or facade; either as a complete habitat or as a stepping stone. A green facade or a terraced structure of a building is not the only possible connection upwards for insects: they can also reach rooftops at various heights via the air. Courtyards and atria are also accessible and can similarly provide a (micro)habitat for insects.

It is furthermore important in a construction plan to survey existing habitats in the immediate vicinity, incorporate them into the plan and strengthen them if possible. Therefore, protect trees, shrubs and other vegetation already present on site as much as possible. From these places, insects can find a green roof or facade more easily, or a cavity made in the wall for this group. Ecological measures in the immediate vicinity of the green roof can also help attract insects. By creating other green elements, such as sections with native plantings, additional shrubs and hedges or blossom-bearing trees nearby, insects can more easily find and colonize the green roof. It is important for insects that the distance between where they live and where they find food is not too great, and that suitable material is available for the eggs and larvae to go through the cycle.

Green structures are also important for another reason: there are a number of bee species (rampion scissor bee, tawny mining bee, honey bee) that use shrubs to create an 'odour plume' that they use to communicate to conspecifics where sources of food are available.

Green roofs or green facades, if of sufficient size, provide a haven for insects. The vegetation on these structures can serve as shelter from predators, extreme temperatures and strong winds. For this, tree stumps can be important, small cavities without water, hiding places in the shade under solar panels or in a crack, and cavities that can be made in the soil on a roof. A green roof does need to be thick enough: thin substrate layers that freeze completely in winter won't provide refuge for insects during that period.

Another important safety issue for insects is light. Many groups of insects are nocturnal, such as moths, caddisflies, beetles and heteropterans. Light pollution is one of the major causes of global insect decline. Excessive lighting at night can disrupt the navigation and reproductive behaviour of insects and expose them too easily to predators.

Complete darkness is most beneficial for nocturnal insects (and for people as well!).

If lighting is really necessary, use subdued lighting with as few lux as possible. Point lighting down rather than up or to the sides. Use a warm colour temperature (such as yellow or orange) which is at least less of a problem than most white and blue light (with lots of UV). Use a motion sensor if lighting is really needed for safety. These lights are still disruptive but at least turn off after a while and are less disruptive than lights that are always on.

For all insects, pesticides are a major problem. Both directly and indirectly. Globally, pesticides are given as one of the main reasons for species decline. In addition, the decline of habitat (in size and quality) plays a strong negative role besides the aforementioned factor of artificial lighting.

Insect safety also has a lot to do with acceptance from residents and users. People readily kill insects (selectively, as they are not likely to do that to butterflies and ladybugs) because they are seen as a nuisance or a threat. Ant killers are still widely used, wasps are controlled with poison, and anti-insect perpend vents are placed in open perpend joints (even where no nuisance is possible). Another considerable

Ecologists from Nijmegen and Krefeld did research in Germany. In 2016 only 25 per cent of the insects were flying about compared to the situation of 27 years ago.

negative factor is pets treated with anti-flea insecticide, which then spread this insecticide outside to vegetation and thus into the insect fauna. It is therefore important to communicate the intrinsic value of insects and the ecosystem services they provide, especially if a green roof or green facade is specifically designed for this purpose. Conveying knowledge and passion about insects and the thinking behind the design can help a building become a real success for species.

Food

The diet of insects can vary widely, from a variety of plant parts (leaves, plant sap, nectar, pollen) to other insects. It depends on the species, life stage and availability of food in their environment. Insects play an important role in food chains and ecosystems by serving as prey animals, herbivores, pollinators and detritivores. When selecting plants on a green roof or facade, preferably choose native plant species that are attractive to various pollinators. People often only think about the flowers, but caterpillars and larvae depend on the foliage of specific plants at their stage, whereas imagoes (adult insects) are often more flexible and can obtain nectar from several plants. Some examples of native species often used in plantings include hemp-agrimony lunaria, winter heath, orpine and aster. In addition, select plants with different flowering periods and make the time between first and last flowering (the 'flowering arch') as long as possible, allowing a greater diversity of species to make use of them throughout the year. Provide a variety of plants that flower or bear berries at different times. A sedum roof is not the preferred option for this reason as it will only flower for a few months a year. Sedum is especially suitable for roofs that have low load-bearing capacity, as the species group requires little substrate (and maintenance).

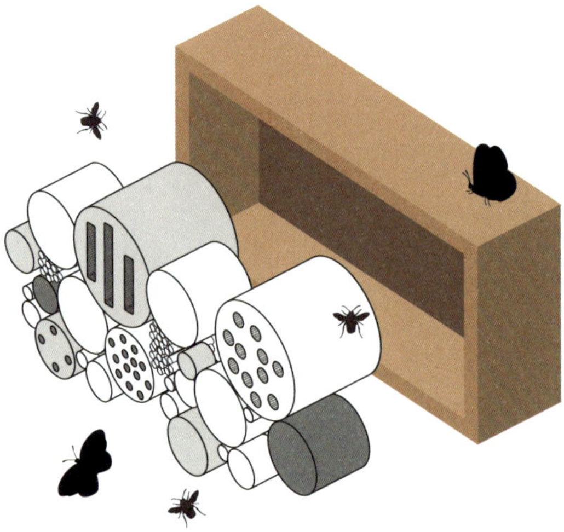

Insect Hotel

- **Dimensions of the openings: 1.5 to 12 mm, smooth on the inside; closed in the back and the tunnels should be 6 to 10 cm deep.**
- **Placement: between 30 cm and 2 meters above the ground. Place the box in a sunny spot and don't place any plants right before the entrances, as they would create shadow and form a hindrance in the flight path.**
- **Materials: wood, stone, clay or bamboo.**

Green roofs that already have flowering plants in spring, such as geranium and chives, will attract more pollinators straight away. When planting in facade systems, planters, and on green roofs, make sure that bedding plants such as lavender have not been cultivated sterile (then they have no pollen), and are preferably grown organically as then they will be plants without (residues of) neonicotinoids, which are disruptive or deadly to insects. On the facade, white bryony or traveller's joy can be used for nectar and pollen for insects. And for all insects that are not flower-visiting but herbivorous, and eat plant material—and in turn are eaten by others.

Predatory insects, including, for example, ladybugs, feed on other insects (such as aphids) and other small organisms living in the green environment, such as insect larvae, mites and snails. Not only the imagoes but also the larvae can be carnivorous, such as the larvae of several species of hoverflies that prey on aphids. Parasitic insects lay eggs in hosts allowing larvae to feed on them and become adults (such as ichneumon wasps on vine weevil), mosquitoes need blood (only the females, when developing eggs). Even dragonflies, provided there is open water nearby, can come to hunt for small insects on a green roof or along a green facade. Ivy can also be a very good species as a facade green. Its inflorescence is liked by all kinds of hoverflies and butterflies until late in the year for nectar and pollen. Some species eat dead plant material (such as beetles feeding on decomposing tree bark and leaf material), others again eat dead animals, and very many insects are herbivores feeding on plant sap, leaves, seeds, pollen and nectar (such as butterflies and bees).

If drought is a risk, plant species that do well on a green roof yet are a bit more resistant to drought and wind, such as sedum rubens and biting stonecrop (sedum species), heather, harebell, greater musk-mallow, catmint, common self-heal and vervain. If the structure allows it, plant berry-bearing and flowering trees and shrubs, such as common barberry, hawthorn and alder buckthorn.

Habitation and Reproduction

Insects need different types of places to stay. An insect hotel or a bee brick is only useful for a small group of insects. Most bees need (loamy) sand or soil to make a

Buggin brick-sized nest box, intended for wild bees and other insects. Bee hotels are suitable for a quarter of the more than 350 species of wild bees in the Netherlands, the other three quarters nest in the ground.

nest. Many insects use perennial vegetation, such as hollow stems or dead wood, to hibernate or lay eggs on or in (which the larvae then live and pupate in). So do not cut everything and do not clear away all dead material, especially hollow stems: there can be a lot of life in uncut grassland. When cutting and disposal of material is indeed necessary, first leave the cut or clipped plant matter for a few days to allow seeds to fall to the soil and any insects to still escape. Many eggs and larvae require the presence of a plant (host plant) on which eggs are deposited and the caterpillars or larvae depend on for food after hatching. Other insects hibernate and find shelter or nesting opportunities in cavities and cracks, between stones or rock piles on a roof, but also in a brick wall or between cracks of stone and/or wooden panelling. It is therefore useful to add natural materials, such as logs or branches, to provide nesting opportunities for solitary bees and other insects. Create options for crawling away such as piles of stones (coarse material with plenty of cavities and recesses). Or place a thick coiled rope that creates a different microclimate underneath, where the material can stay moist for longer and help insects.

For a self-designed insect hotel or insect block, make sure to make holes from small to large, roughly between 1.5 mm and 12 mm. Very important here is that you drill with a very sharp drill bit, the edges and drill passage should be very smooth to avoid damaging insect wings. Preferably orient the hotel or the masonry bee bricks towards the south, south-east or south-west, and not in the shade.

For reproduction, insects use different ways to find each other, depending on the species and their specific behaviour. These can include odour (butterflies), sound (grasshoppers) or flight patterns (dagger flies). In all cases, it is important that the partners can find each other and pick up the signals.

Building height is not likely to be the limiting factor for insect diversity on a roof. Studies have shown that insects still occur even at a height of 70 metres, although success does depend on the volume of the substrate. The higher the roof, the thicker the substrate and the better the sheltering from wind and sun should be. Bees and wasps

Tawny mining bee / Red-tailed bumblebee / Hoverfly.

are somewhat less likely to use these heights, while flies, butterflies and hoverflies have much less trouble doing so.

Species Groups

The insect world is vast and tremendously diverse. It is impossible, and also less relevant in the context of nature-inclusive building, to discuss all species groups in detail. The overview below is limited to those species groups found in facade greenery and roof gardens, and for which nature-inclusive measures can be taken. Of course, we share our buildings with many more invertebrates such as spiders (pseudeuophrys lanigera, scytodes thoracica), mites (house dust mites) and wingless insects such as the silverfish. There are also many soil species (on green roofs) and common species of flies, ants, springtails and heteropterans, all of which are also known to be users of building facades and roofs, but it is beyond the scope of this book to elaborate on these.

Bees

Bees are one of the most highly appreciated insect species at the moment: much attention is being paid to this group. It is often said that 'the bee' is not doing well—but 'the' bee does not exist. There is a difference in lifestyle between social bees that live in groups, such as the honey bee and bumblebees, and solitary bees, such as the red mason bee. Bees pollinate flowers and plants, contributing to the reproduction and conservation of various plant species.

Bees can nest both aboveground and underground, with some species being able to do both. In relation to buildings, bees can build nests in cavities, such as holes in walls or between bricks. In addition, nesting opportunities can be found in dead wood (European orchard bee and leaf-cutter bee), loamy or sandy soil (like the hairy-footed flower bee), and hollow stems (like the common yellow-faced bee). To help these bees, bee hotels can be installed, such as wooden or brick nesting blocks with holes of varying diameters to attract a variety of species. However, the majority of bees need sandy or loamy soil to make a ground nest in. Only a small proportion of wild bees are helped by an insect hotel. Variation in substrate depth of a green roof, but also the 'brown roof', holds potential for ground-nesting species. The buff-tailed bumblebee nests on the ground in burrows of mice. On roofs, you will rarely if ever come across these, which is why it is important for this and also other species to be able to get between 5-50 cm deep into the soil, where the material is not too stony.

There are about 350 species of wild bees in the Netherlands, many of which are on the Red List. Here, it is important to prevent suitable sites and habitats from disappearing too quickly as a result of clearance or (temporary) landscaping. To illustrate: the

Common brimstone / Anthophora quadrimaculata / Admiral butterfly.

common dandelion and various flowering willows are enormously useful plants for bees. Suitable sites should have flowering plants available that are mowed in phases and have warm, sunlit soil for nesting. And it cannot be said often enough: avoid sowing with all kinds of flower mixtures. It is not necessary for insects and is often accompanied by flora adulteration, and thus can even be counterproductive for some species. Spontaneous vegetation and proper monitoring with maintenance is best for insect conservation.
What should also be avoided in nature-inclusive building is the placement of honey bee hives. These have a demonstrated negative effect on the occurrence of wild bees, as they create unnatural competition. So please do install insect hotels for wild bees and not hives for honey bees.

Bumblebees
The group of bees also includes bumblebees. Bumblebees are social bees and, notably, look a bit different, in that they tend to be hairier and a bit larger. Bumblebees have a special adaptation that allows them to open the flower buds of certain plants by vibrating their wings, a process known as 'buzz pollination'. This makes bumblebees a special kind of pollinator for many plant species, for which this way of pollination is very efficient. Bumblebees usually form smaller colonies in small burrows in the ground, such as an old mousehole. But they may also nest in a cavity wall, under a floor or in a special bumblebee hive on a green roof. However, experience with bumblebee hives is limited; a ground nest remains the preferred choice for this species. Common bumblebees are the carder bumblebee, buff-tailed bumblebee and garden bumblebee.

Hoverflies
Hoverflies, of which there are about 350 species in the Netherlands, sometimes look like small bees or wasps, but are actually flies. They are less well known than bees, but are just as important as pollinators and they play a role in controlling harmful insects. So hoverflies need flowering plants with nectar and pollen. Hoverflies do not make a nest. Depending on the species, eggs are laid on plants (after which the larvae forage on aphids) or in rotting wood or hollow stems. Common species found on green roofs include the common compost fly and migrant aphid eater.

Butterflies
Most people see butterflies, of which there are 53 species in the Netherlands, as the most beautiful insects that can also be spotted in urban areas. Butterflies play an important role in pollinating flowers. Many butterfly species have specific host plants on

which they lay their eggs and on which the caterpillars feed: an essential animal-plant relationship for reproduction. In some species, this relationship is quite close: for example, a brimstone butterfly needs alder buckthorn or purging buckthorn, while peacock butterfly, map, and small tortoiseshell use common nettles to deposit eggs on, and common blue in turn wants clovers (black medick and bird's-foot trefoil, for example). To attract butterflies, native plants that serve as food sources and host plants for their caterpillars are needed. A sunny spot with shelter is the ideal habitat for butterflies: herb-rich grassland with structural variation is what this species group needs, just like many other insects. Common species in the city include small and large white, peacock butterfly, comma, holly blue, red admiral, green-veined white and speckled wood.
A special butterfly hotel for hibernation does exist, but whether it is useful is debatable. Focusing on sufficient food and structural variation in terms of vegetation will suffice. Many butterflies spend the winter as eggs or pupae, but species such as peacock and comma also spend the winter as butterflies (the imago). They then hang in a shed, in a tree cavity or even in an underground bunker or cellar. In the Netherlands, there are some butterfly species that migrate to other areas in winter. The best-known migrant butterfly species is the red admiral. This butterfly species migrates south in autumn, towards warmer regions, such as southern Europe and North Africa. Some painted ladies do the same. They do not return to the Netherlands until spring.

Moths
Moths belong to the order Lepidoptera, just like butterflies. Lifestyle is the main difference between moths and butterflies. Moths are mainly active at night, while butterflies fly during the day. There is a huge variety in shapes, colours and sizes, with more than 2,500 species in the Netherlands alone. The antennae of moths are more feathery (slimmer in butterflies with a small ball at the end). Those feathered antennae are needed to detect pheromones and scents: they use them to find mates, to communicate and also to smell food from a distance. Developing a natural vegetation type such as thickets or herb-rich grassland is the best way to help moths (and nature in general). Moths play a major role in flower pollination and are an important food source for diurnal and nocturnal animals, such as several species of bats. The caterpillars of the mottled umber are the main food for tits' nests in woodland areas in spring. Nocturnal butterflies are particularly sensitive to light pollution. Common moths in urban areas include brimstone moth, silver Y, large yellow underwing and dark strawberry tortrix. Plants suitable for moths and fragrant at night include evening primrose, dame's violet, camomile and honeysuckle. It is important to note here that these are just a few examples and are not universal for the species group: it is important that a large volume of plants is present for both flower-visiting and herbivorous species, in other words a variation that approaches natural vegetation as much as possible.

Micros
Micros, derived from the word 'microlepidoptera', are a collection of butterfly families that usually belong to the smallest category of butterflies. The classification 'macro' and 'micro' is mainly pragmatic, although sometimes the older butterfly families are grouped under micros. Micros too can have a distinctive wing pattern. With their limited size, they

Insect hotel / Large yellow underwing / Brimstone moth.

are just somewhat less conspicuous than the larger diurnal or macro butterflies. Micros contribute to pollination (albeit to a limited extent) and are prey for other animals. This group can be both diurnal and nocturnal, depending on the species. The horse-chestnut leafminer, lime bentwing and large fruit-tree tortrix are examples of micros in the city.

Beetles

Beetles are the largest insect group in the world, and logically their diversity is enormous. They determine much of the species diversity on earth. The Netherlands has more than 4,000 species. A great diversity can also be found in cities. Beetles have different lifestyles and can be found on land and in fresh water. Some beetle species, such as leaf beetles, feed on leaves of plants. Others, such as ground beetles, are active hunters that catch and eat other small animals: the carabus granulatus is one such species in the city. Beetles also play an important role in decomposing organic matter. The larvae of some beetle families eat dead plant material or remains of dead animals (carrion beetles such as the common sexton beetle), playing an important role in recycling nutrients in the ecosystem. Also, beetles themselves in turn serve as food sources for many animals, such as birds and mammals.

Of all the beetles, ladybugs are probably the best known and most 'likeable' group. They even symbolize non-violence in all kinds of media statements these days. And they are a popular beetle species because they are known to control aphids (so the species provides an ecosystem service to us humans). There are nesting boxes on the market in which ladybugs can also hibernate, often combined with an insect hotel. A number of slots are needed (both horizontal and vertical) and in the abode some twigs, hay or stems for insulation and to crawl under.

There are beetle species that can nest in crevices, cracks and under eaves of buildings. To help beetles thrive, there are several options, depending on the species group. Varied and natural planting can provide suitable habitat. In an herb- or shrub-rich thicket, the adult beetles find food such as prey animals and there is plenty of flower supply. In addition, host plants and accumulation of organic material provide a beetle-attractive environment. The hawthorn leaf beetle, grammoptera ruficornis and bronze carabid are examples of beetles in the city. Like butterflies, beetles pupate. This makes them vulnerable in terms of landscape management: they cannot escape the mower. Therefore, it is best to phase management and allow shrub or thicket vegetation to develop naturally.

Buildings for animals

Since the dawn of agriculture, people have built pens and stables for domestic animals at their settlements. Traditional building techniques also unintentionally provided space for other animals that lived with us, such as barn owls, house sparrows and bats. Much more recently, people started facilitating accommodation spaces for wild animals as well. This has led to constructions exclusively for animals, such as insect hotels, house martin cotes, house sparrow flats and bat towers.

A special structure for animals is particularly important if shelter or nesting facilities disappear when new buildings are built or existing ones are modified. For example, when insulation measures in existing dwellings change the heat and moisture balance, resulting in a loss of habitat quality for bats or birds.

Another reason for erecting structures for specific animal species is the legal requirement for compensatory measures in case of demolition. A purpose-built structure can thus provide an alternative habitat (temporary or otherwise) if the original habitat disappears with demolition.

A third reason may be that there is plenty of food available in the area, but no places to roost or nest. Adding a structure specifically for animals places the 'hotel' closer to the 'restaurant', as it were, such as an insect hotel a short distance from flowering plants.

The disadvantage of a structure made exclusively for animals is that such objects must be able to function entirely independently. They need their own foundation, construction, cladding and sometimes even water supply or heating. The object cannot benefit from facilities that are already available in a building intended for humans. At the same time, the advantage is that it does not have to be integrated into the building itself, which simplifies the construction process and usually gives more freedom in terms of design.

The Ecolumn is a prefab building kit for stackable nest boxes. Accommodations for the common sparrow, house martin, common swift, jackdaw, starling, stock dove, and other songbirds that roost in cavities. But also for the little owl, barn owl, kestrel, stork and various species of bats, honeybees and solitary bees. (Ecolumn, Faunus Nature Creations, 2022, NL)

The Bat Tower stands like a sculpture in the Griffis sculpture park. A three-dimensional cave with an excess of openings accommodates bats. It also serves as a call to protect bats and preserve their vanishing habitat in the city. (Bat Tower, Buffalo NY, Joyce Hwang, 2021, US)

Built from debris and branches it accommodates both animals and plants. (Fauna wall, Almere, Utopia Island, 2020, NL)

The design is inspired by the silhouette of the common swift in flight. The stainless-steel structure features a tiered rack with modular drawers measuring 320 x 220 x 290 mm with a total of 90 nesting chambers. The tower also functions as a lighting element and city sculpture. (Swift tower, Warsaw, Menthol architects, 2013, PL)

Aeres Hogeschool

Almere, BDG Architecten, 2021, NL

This school building not only contains classrooms but is also a research object for the students in nature development and food supply. The plants and the insects and birds that descend on them are part of the learning environment. In addition to green roofs and facades, the building also has a green interior.

The facades of the building have a different design for each orientation. On the west side, the facade features semi-transparent solar panels that also serve as sunshades. The green facades on the east side incorporate nest boxes and a bee ladder. This plant-assisted line allows bees to move to higher parts of the building. The roof is herbaceous and the terraces are decorated with planters with native plants. The rooftop garden substrate matches the soil type in the surrounding area to make it easier for soil life, and hence native flora and fauna, to connect to the immediate environment.

The interior planting winds from the entrance to the top of the building. The greenery is intended to regulate the indoor climate and provide a pleasant learning environment. To guide the greenery both in, on and on the building, a computer-controlled watering system was installed. Through an extensive network of hoses, the plants are supplied with water and nutrients. The building and the greenery also have an educational function; for instance, monitoring is partly carried out together with the college's students.

Right: Green facade with computer-controlled irrigation system / Bee ladder / Nest box / The building was part of the agricultural exhibition Expo Floriade 2022 / Below: The planting in the interior winds upwards from the entrance to the top of the building.

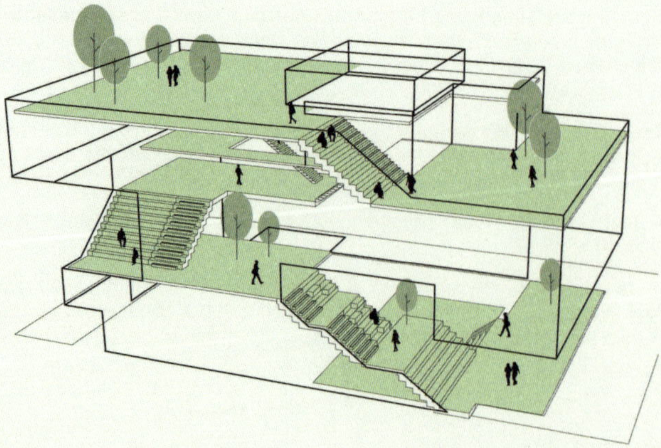

Building & Birds

Birds are among the most striking animal species in the city; everyone can name a few of them. Whether you know them by name or not, most people enjoy birdsong and are able to hear whether or not there is a diversity of species in an area by the different calls and melodies. The variety of species is indeed great, both globally and within a city. Cities can host a great diversity of bird species, especially during bird migration in spring and autumn. Of these species, about a hundred breed in the city in the Netherlands, the rest are migrants who use the city as a short stopover, or are exclusively winter or summer visitors.

We have long shared our buildings with birds; some species are counted among the 'hemerophiles'. These are the birds that can benefit from human activity and adapt to the human-made environment. So they change with us—but can also suffer from changes we make if this happens at too fast a pace.
Jackdaws, feral pigeons and house sparrows are among the best-known bird species in cities. They use built-up areas right into the centre of cities, taking advantage of food left behind by people in addition to the natural food available. Species thus exploit the opportunities offered by the city, seeking conditions similar to those of their natural habitat. For example, birds that are more or less building-bound will often have rock-dwelling origins. The best-known example is the feral pigeon, but on flat roofs you will also find birds that usually live in, for instance, grasslands. Such as, for example, the oystercatcher, which originally breeds on gravel beaches. For them, flat roofs with gravel, shells or other coarse material now make good alternative nesting sites.
Species that were previously on the verge of extinction have also returned precisely because they have discovered the city as a habitat. The peregrine falcon was almost extinct in the 1970s mainly due to agricultural toxins, but the species is now recovering and has discovered the city as a new territory.

Food and Reproduction
Most urban birds—except birds of prey—feed on insects, seeds and berries. They find that food supply from vegetation on and around buildings, partly because of the supply of berries and seeds, but also because of the presence of insects around this vegetation. Native plantings are preferred here because they attract native insects and provide a lot of known edible material for birds. Non-native plants will attract far fewer insects because they are not used to them. A key factor here is not to use insecticides: these enter the food chain and, besides killing insects, have a negative effect on the

Starling at Rotterdam Central Station.

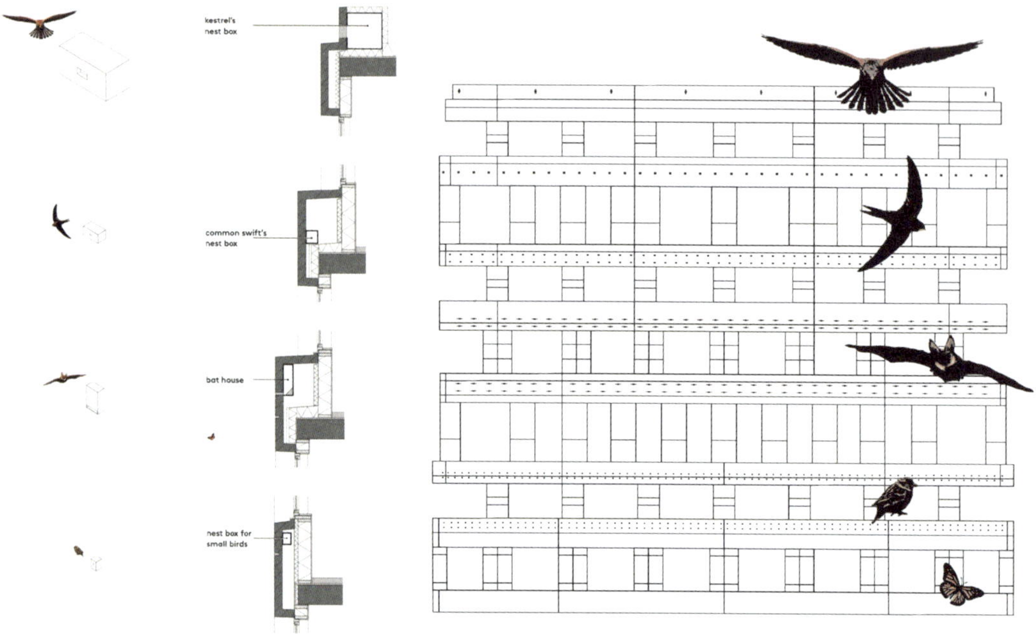

The Rock is part of Vertical, an ensemble of four buildings in the Amsterdam Sloterdijk neighbourhood. In addition to housing people, the Rock will also house birds and bats.

Special nest bricks and shelters were designed for the coloured bands in the facade. Together with the gardens on the adjacent residential high-rise (NL Architects) a habitat is created for bees, butterflies, bats, small city birds, common swifts and falcons. The Rock functions as a 'hotel' in all this and the high green residential high-rise as the 'restaurant'. The earth-coloured, horizontal lineation of the monolithic building references the layers found in rock formations. ((De Rots, Vertical, Amsterdam, Studio Donna van Milligen Bielke, 2023, NL)

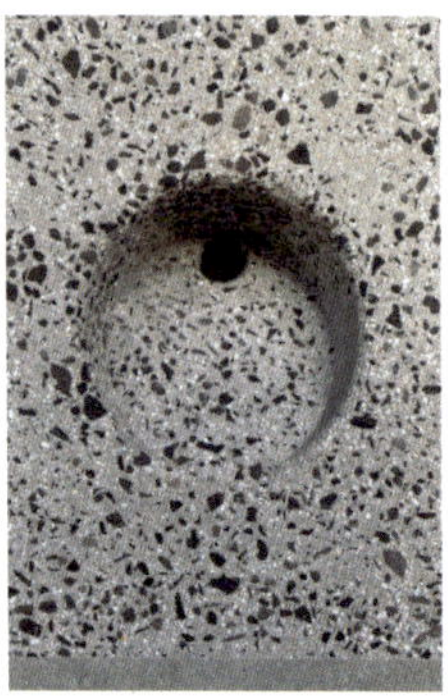

food supply for birds as well as on their health. For birds of prey such as the peregrine falcon, there must be sufficient prey: in other words, a healthy bird population in the urban area. Even for species that are not building-bound, the building can perform a function for food or as a temporary shelter. Tree-dwelling bird species can equally come to forage on a green roof.

All birds need water nearby. Not only for drinking but also for bathing. Most birds will find this water in the vicinity. Making open water on a roof can lead to a mosquito problem and is not recommended (apart from the problem that a water dish will evaporate very quickly on hot days). Do provide a sand pile on the roof, as birds usually take a dry bath to clean off excess grease. These features can be added on a green roof, on terraces or at the base of the building.

The place where birds breed often coincides with that of their general habitat and/or nesting sites. Most birds find each other through songs and calls. Males also use these to mark their territory. Generally, spring is the breeding season for birds and after the eggs are laid, they are often incubated by both the female and the male. The incubation period varies by species and ranges from days to weeks. Some bird species breed several times a season. The incubation period is a vulnerable time for birds, as is the time that follows when the chicks have hatched and need food that the parents must constantly supply. During this period, the chicks need to get plenty of protein to grow, and they have to be sufficiently sheltered from weather and enemies. Humans are one such enemy, as they can undertake disruptive activities. At the same time, people can also do the opposite and provide many conditions for successful reproduction by providing nesting opportunities, food and safety.

To facilitate birds living on and around a building, it is necessary to create cavities in the facade or include built-in boxes in the design. Only if this is not possible should nest boxes be considered. The opening of cavities or nest boxes can be restrictive. The size of the opening determines which species can use it, and for some species the shape is also important. Small birds prefer small openings because that way large birds cannot reach the nest to rob it, or to occupy it, causing the smaller birds to lose out. Since several bird species may compete with each other for the same nest site, it is wise to provide a diverse range of nesting opportunities large enough for all bird species.

Roosts

Birds find places to roost both on the building (the roof), attached to the building (in wall vegetation) and inside the building (in crevices, cracks, the cavity or under roof tiles). Due to the porosity of the building, the birds see it as an attractive rock wall with advantages such as more warmth, a more stable climate, conveniently high, free of predators and close to food sources left or planted by humans. As such traditional habitats disappear with new construction methods, it is important in nature-inclusive building to add those spaces again, thus providing habitat for birds.

All built-in features, such as nest boxes, come at the expense of the regular insulation layer. A higher-quality piece of insulation must therefore be made at the back to maintain the desired insulation value and prevent a thermal bridge. For fire-sensitive structures, it is also important to ensure that the built-in unit does not undermine the fire safety rating. Openings of all nest boxes should be placed at least half a metre from windows and doors. Because of the risk of overheating, it is not wise to install nest boxes on the south facade, unless the facade section is nearly always in the shade nonetheless. North, east or north-east orientation is preferred.

Connections

The importance of green connections for highly mobile species such as birds varies between scales. Many birds migrate and use connections at a very high scale level. Common swifts, house martins, lesser black-backed gulls and black redstarts migrate south to Africa. Eurasian oystercatchers and European herring gulls move to coastal areas, while species such as the house sparrow stay very close to home throughout the year.

At a smaller scale, for example during the breeding season, many birds depend on habitats immediately around the building and this can be expressed in metres. It is important to have functioning connections, the 'green' and 'blue' routes through the city, from the roosts to the foraging areas. Precisely because the area of green space in the city is relatively small, green connections are an important part of the habitat of species and are a determining factor for settlement. The connections can also be used as shelter, roosting and foraging areas themselves: a connection need not only go from A to B, the line-shaped element is in itself important as an area for many species.

Birds forage throughout the city. Therefore, even an isolated green roof in the city centre can serve as a stepping stone for birds roaming the city in search of food or a place to rest and take shelter. The city itself can also be a stopover on a larger scale, during migration, and is thus part of the connection for birds.

Threats

Urban birds seek out cities because of the advantages, including safety. There are many different places to shelter, there is relatively less use of (agricultural) toxins and some of their natural enemies are often absent. At the same time, the city poses just as many risks. These are in particular human disturbance or even destruction of habitats, buildings with glass as a collision risk, lighting and predation by pets such as the domestic cat. Disturbance by humans need not always be active, simply our presence can also cause stress, making breeding less successful. Particularly in an urban area, it is therefore important to find a balance and ensure sufficient green areas with peace and quiet, low levels of human presence, and darkness, also for birds.

Species

This chapter deals with the most common urban birds that have a certain degree of site fidelity and use the building itself. A selection has therefore been made, and general garden species are not discussed if they have no relation with a building itself.

House Sparrow

House sparrows are among the most common building-dwelling birds in the city. They live in loose colonies. Their food consists of seeds, grains, insects, flower buds and berries, supplemented by food provided by humans, such as breadcrumbs, peanuts, and fat balls. During the period when they have chicks, the parents eat mainly insects.

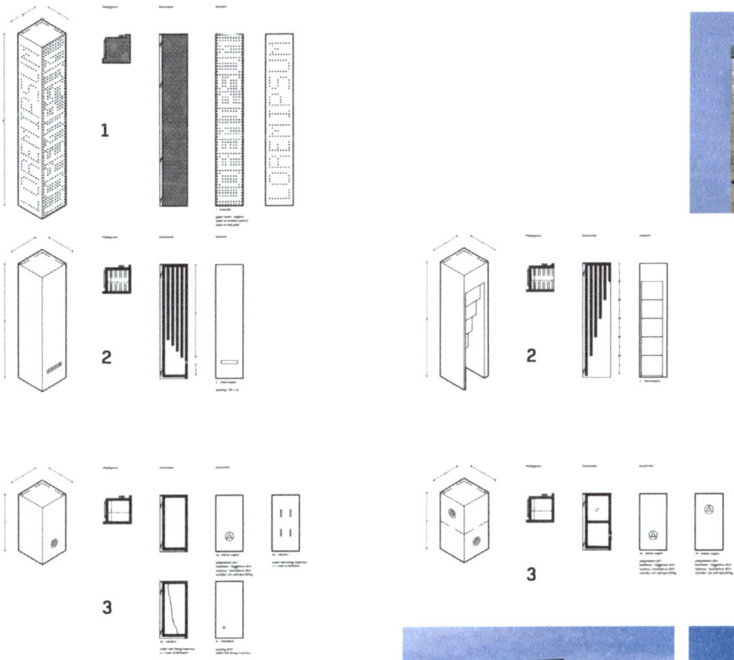

1. INSECTS
2. BATS
3. SMALL BIRDS, BUTTERFLIES, BUMBLEBEES
4. LITTLE OWL, SWIFTS
5. KESTREL

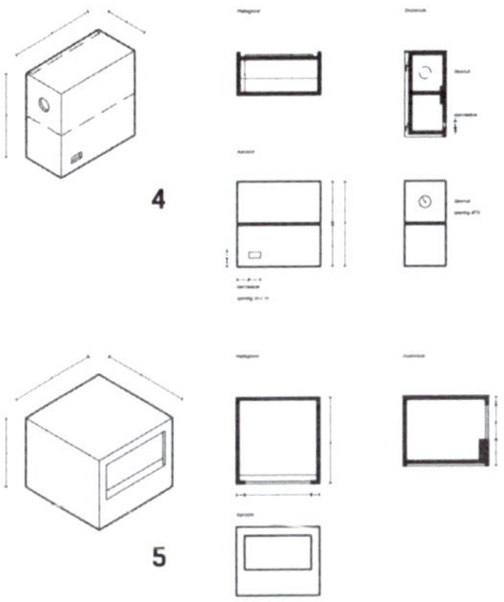

The animal tree is a 'residential tower' for insects, birds and bats. There are four of these landmarks along the Poelzone in the Westland region in the southwest of the Netherlands. Using modular box elements, a different tower was assembled for each location. Jackdaws, sparrows, and even a kestrel have already been spotted. (Animal tree: Municipality of Westland, Finnbarr McComb Architecten, LOLA Landscape Architects and Aqua Terra Nova, 2016, NL)

The house sparrow is also a hemerophile and eats people's food around terraces, public transport stations, and in places where people shake out their tablecloths or feed the birds. It also finds food in herb-rich roadsides, the 'weeds' in the streets or in tree beds. Half-paving at ground level, green facades and green roofs can provide an additional food supply for the house sparrow close to its nest.
House sparrows used to roost under roof tiles but also in wall cavities. But these days, they need our help. House sparrows sometimes nest with dozens of pairs in a small area and seek their nesting places in our buildings. It is therefore important for

This educational building is located as a bridge over a reconstructed wetland on the tree-lined campus of Vassar College. To prevent bird collisions with the glass, a number of measures were taken. At the main level, which offers views into the verdant landscape, Ornilux glass has been used. The spiderweb-like Ornilux pattern is almost invisible to the human eye, but is recognizable to birds.

The upper levels have slats, and a tree pattern was imprinted on the glass. This pattern is visible to birds in all daylight conditions and has the added advantage of shading the interior. (Bridge for Laboratory Sciences, Vassar College, Poughkeepsie, Ennead Architects, 2016, US)

the house sparrow that at least five, or better still ten, nest boxes are placed together, preferably at a height of 6 metres (eaves height) or just below and at a maximum height of 15 metres. The opening of a box should be about 35 mm, with a floor area of 15x15 cm and a height of about 22 cm. The box should be placed on a north or east orientation.

The nest boxes can be used year-round, so not just when there are young, but also the rest of the year, especially during cold periods. Additionally, evergreen shrubs are used as roosting and hiding places. House sparrows are sedentary and as a group have a small action radius. Life during the breeding season, from roughly early March through July, takes place within a circle of about 50 to a maximum of 200 metres around the nest. Even after swarming out, the young birds travel no further than a kilometre to find a territory of their own. Shelter can be provided by planting shrubs that remain evergreen, no more than 50 metres away from the nest box and roost site.

Planting that supports the habitat of house sparrows: wall vegetation (such as ivy, vine), hedges such as privet, shrubs that are impenetrable such as holly/fire thorn and ligneous species such as hawthorn. When carrying out maintenance work, it is important not to prune back everything at once, but parts of it every other year.

Common Swift

Swifts spend most of their lives in the air and sleep there too, except during the breeding season when they spend the night on the nest. They even mate in the air. Swifts eat insects above water or vegetation; but mostly high in the sky and around their own nest site. They have a range of several kilometres for finding their food. Moisture is taken from food, but also in full flight from puddles and lakes. The only time they descend and need a building is to make a nest, incubate eggs and fledge the young. Specific connections to the building environment are not really necessary, they continue to get their food from the air.

Swifts breed in May and June, and are colony breeders. Therefore, at least five nesting sites should be located in close proximity to each other. They make their nest in available niches and cavities in buildings; under the gutter, behind the drainpipe, dormer, roof tile, in voids under an overhang, or in a hole in the wall. Such places can be located up to 40 metres high. If these are not available—in newer buildings—special masonry bricks can be provided.

For built-in boxes, high, blind walls with a good approach route are most suitable, also because of the free fall. The entrance opening should be oval, 3 cm high and 6.5 cm wide, and the box should have a minimum size of 25 cm wide, 15 cm deep and 13 cm high. The swift returns to the same site where they were successful every year. Because of this site fidelity, new nest boxes have a particularly good chance of success when placed on or near an already (or previously) existing site.

In the past, common swift roof tiles were regularly used, but due to insulation under the roof, they are no longer placed nowadays, as there is a risk of overheating the nest. In the case of common swifts, decoy sounds are also played to help them discover a new nesting opportunity more quickly.

Common swifts migrate to Africa from mid-July and return from the last days of April. This makes them one of the shortest staying breeding birds in the Netherlands.

House sparrow/ House martin / Black redstart.

House Martin

House martins are migratory birds that arrive to nest in May and migrate to Africa in September. They live in colonies and have high site fidelity; their nests are used every year. Their range is about 500 metres around the nest. They look for their food—flying insects such as flies and mosquitoes—mostly over water, so a water-rich environment is important. House martins nest in semi-circular bowls under gutters or protruding eaves. The building is essential for this species as they attach their nests to a wall. This nest is built of mud, the birds make little balls of mud that they keep sticking together until a bowl is created, but you can also provide artificial nests. Favourite spots are where walls meet with cantilevered building sections or beams, so nests can be built in the 'axils'.
The house martin favours white: almost exclusively white gutters and overhangs are accepted as nest sites. Crossbars are almost essential for a nest to be permanently anchored; nests with little lateral support are more likely to be lost. Acceptance of a site is also most likely if nests are already present nearby. The height is at least 4 metres and the nest has a good approach route, with no obstacles in the form of trees in front of the eaves. House martin cotes are also installed separately from the building, but in practice these prove less effective than those attached to a building. For house martins, it is essential to have mud with clay available, often in the urban fringes in farmyards or fields with clay, or near ponds.

Black Redstart

The black redstart is a migratory bird that increasingly winters in the Netherlands due to the changing climate. Its diet consists largely of insects, but it also eats seeds and berries. The favourite habitat of the black redstart is a fallow area, or next to or on a so-called brown roof (grit of rubble with some sand and some coarse material such as some larger pieces of stone, possibly also a mixture with some shells and even tree bark). So not in a very green environment; some spontaneous growth is fine, such as succulents and other drought- and heat-resistant species. Nest boxes should be placed on their own; the species is not a colony breeder. It is good to hang a few boxes on a building, though, a pair will eventually pick one. The dimensions of the box should measure about 16x16 cm floor area and 16 cm high with a semi-circular opening of 13x6 cm. Hang the box at a height of more than 2 metres, on (green) brown roofs up to 20 metres (maximum 30 metres) high. The birds sing from the eaves or the highest part of a gabled roof.

Common Starling

Outside the breeding season, the starling lives in groups, and it nests in tree cavities as

A flock of starlings over Rotterdam.

well as in cavities in buildings. The nests are used only during the breeding season and not at other times of the year. The starling feeds on insects and insect larvae found in meadows and lawns, but supplements this diet with berries and seeds in bushes in autumn. It likes to forage close to its nest, on lawns to look for insect larvae. Preferably within 500 metres of the nest. Besides open grassland, the starling needs bushes and trees for shelter and rest.

Nest boxes for starlings have a size of about 16x16 cm surface area and 30 cm height, with a round hole of about 45 mm as an entrance opening. Place five boxes together at a height of 3 to 5 metres, maximum 10 metres, with the boxes hanging in the shade. Apart from buildings, the boxes can also be attached to tree trunks.

Eurasian Oystercatcher

Originally a coastal breeding bird, the oystercatcher is now increasingly found on flat gravel roofs in the city. In urban areas, it feeds on insects and insect larvae, so it needs grasslands and lawns in the area to find them. Oystercatchers, as well as common terns and some gull species, nest in the city on roofs with pebbles or shells (a special gravel bin if necessary), or on a brown roof with a patch of gravel or crushed rubble. Oystercatchers benefit from a substrate layer of several centimetres so that they can make a nesting hole. In addition, there should be an eave high enough so that chicks cannot fall directly off the roof. Placing a hollow pipe is recommended so that chicks can hide from predators and seek shelter from overly bright sun or precipitation. Roof height up to 15 metres. One option is to combine facilities for the oystercatcher with solar panels on the roof. These also provide the necessary shelter next to the open area where the birds can nest.

A colourful collection of nest boxes for birds as an art project.

Gulls

The lesser black-backed gull and herring gull are both coastal birds, but can also be found in cities. They also forage on litter in cities, causing nuisance. Especially during the breeding season, they can search for food up to tens of kilometres from the nest. The lesser black-backed gull is a migratory bird that arrives in March and, like the herring gull, breeds in May. Both seek a nesting site free of predators. They are ground-breeders but in the city, they usually look for a place on a roof as it is safer there. The roof may consist of gravel or crushed rubble. A nest is often made near some relief, such as next to a chimney. It is useful to provide hiding places for the young, such as a (sewer) pipe or pallet, for protection against the weather but also against predators (a crow coming to snatch a chick). Not going on the roof during the breeding season prevents unnecessary disturbance. A bitumen roof is likely to get too hot, and a roof with a high raised eave may not be safe enough for these species because they may not perceive threats sufficiently early. It is important that window cleaning or work on the roof does not take place during the breeding season.

Tits

Great tits and blue tits eat berries, caterpillars and insects, as well as seeds found in trees and bushes. Tits make a nest in all kinds of cavities, in both trees and buildings. They like to use nest boxes. Tits need a green environment such as a garden nearby. They are not colony animals, so place solitary boxes at 10-metre intervals. Dimensions

Starling / Oystercatcher / Common swift.

of the box 12x12 cm surface area and 32 cm height. Great tits require a round entrance opening of 32 mm diameter, blue tits one of 28 mm diameter.

Peregrine Falcon

The peregrine falcon is a bird of prey that can also use a highly urbanized area as its habitat. In the city, it finds feral pigeons, jackdaws, starlings and, nowadays, quite a few rose-ringed parakeets. Peregrine falcons are territorial and defend their hunting area of several hundred metres around their nest. They find their nesting sites in a variety of places: outside the city, this may be a nest on the ground, but in the city, high ledges on buildings and churches, a high-voltage pylon or a mast are used. The peregrine falcon returns to the same site every year. They do not nest on the buildings themselves, but often use a nest box provided for the species. The breeding success is then a lot higher than when the eggs are laid on eaves. A peregrine falcon box should ideally be 80 cm wide, 62 cm high and 64 cm deep. Provide a grid for landing and line the box with fine gravel that is not sharp. A box should preferably be placed at 80 metres high in a place where no people come. It is essential that the box can be reached for maintenance (annual cleaning) and the ringing of possible chicks for research. Again, it is important to refrain from window cleaning or work on the roof during the breeding season. When considering placing a nest box, it should first be analysed whether there are already boxes in the area, so as not to place too many. Given the wide territorial distance, it makes no sense to install multiple boxes on buildings that are a relatively short distance apart. Consult a bird expert for this.

Other Species

A number of species in relation to the building are not mentioned separately, but are mentioned here. These include the short-toed treecreeper, white wagtail, blackbird and feral pigeon.

Treecreepers, like tits, occur in crevices and cavities provided by a building. Treecreepers primarily need trees to forage and search for insects and spiders. A special nest box for treecreepers, with a side entrance on the wall side can be added to a building. The white wagtail can also use special nest boxes for this species on buildings.

Blackbirds are known to favour nesting in wall greenery such as ivy. A dense cover of ivy, for example, provides the sturdiness for a nest and protection from both the weather and enemies. Providing this facade greenery is a stimulating measure for this species, and it goes without saying that pruning should be done outside the breeding season.

Nest boxes

Buildings before 1980 contained numerous nesting and sheltering options for birds in cracks and cavities in the facade and space under the roof tiles. These openings have disappeared due to new building methods. Therefore, integrating nest boxes is necessary to preserve building-bound bird species in our living environment.

As a rule, birds are rather picky. For instance, in terms of nest location, each species has specific preferences when it comes to the height on the building, the inside dimensions of the nest box and the entrance opening.

For nest boxes, south-facing orientation is generally not recommended due to the risk of overheating in summer. However, if they are shaded by, for example, a nearby tree or adjacent buildings, south and west facades may also be suitable.

For colony birds, such as the house sparrow and common swift, it is important to place several boxes together. Proximity to greenery for shelter is also crucial. Sparrows, for instance, benefit from a hedge a short distance from their nests.

The openings of a bird's box will determine quite precisely whether a species will accept the box, can enter it by itself (the cross-section of the skull is usually normative) while larger species, on the other hand, cannot fit through it. A low box for a great tit, for example, does not work because this bird stacks a lot of nesting material. A house swallow nest box will only work if it is installed under an eaves or gutter. The common swift does not stack and wants the entrance opening to be low, but not too low as the young might fall out.

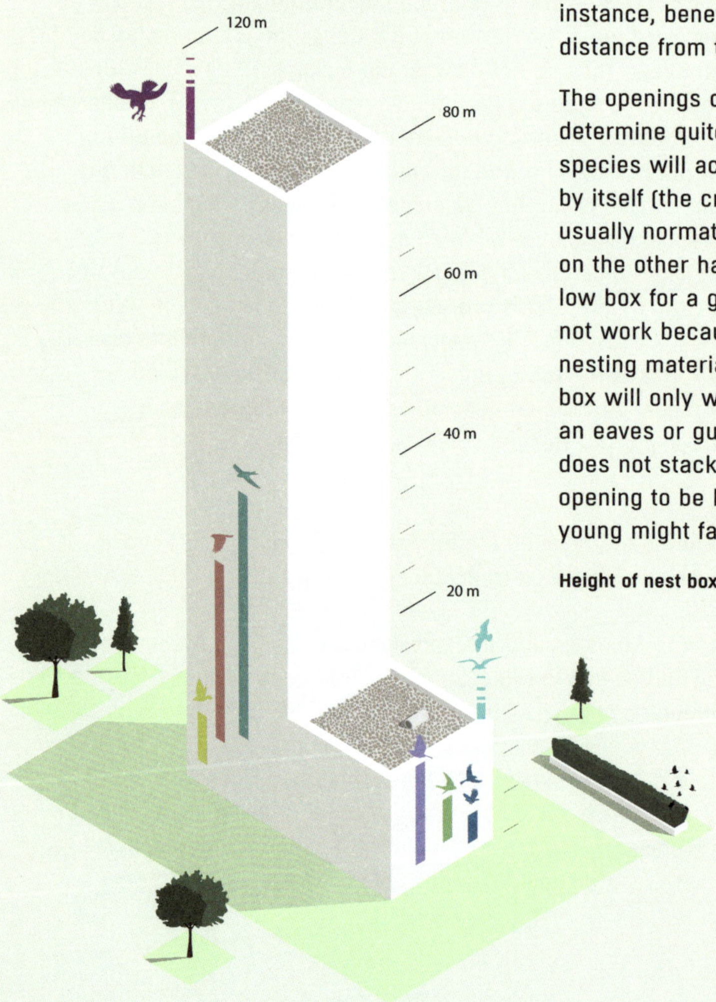

Height of nest boxes per species.

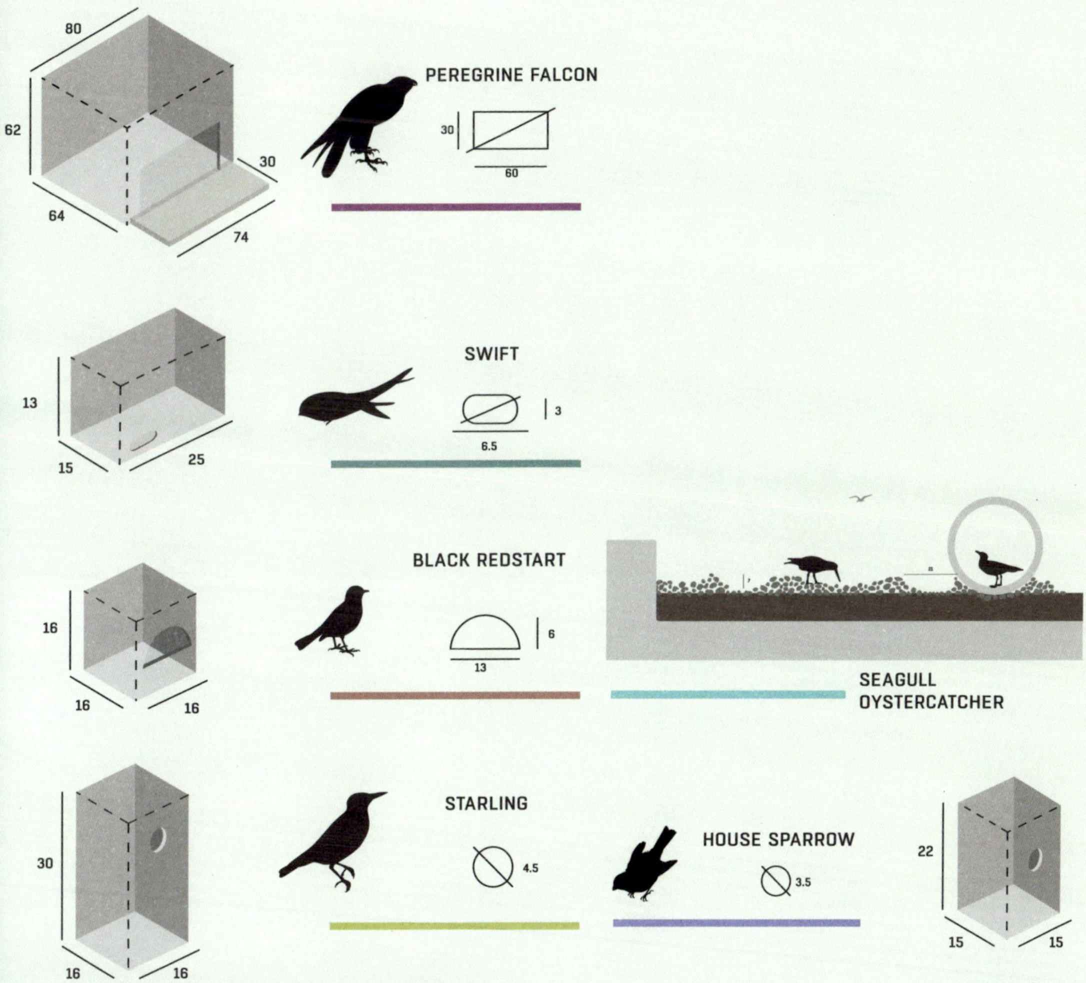

Nest boxes for tits, house sparrows and starlings can be placed on the southwest if there is shade from a nearby tree or adjacent buildings.

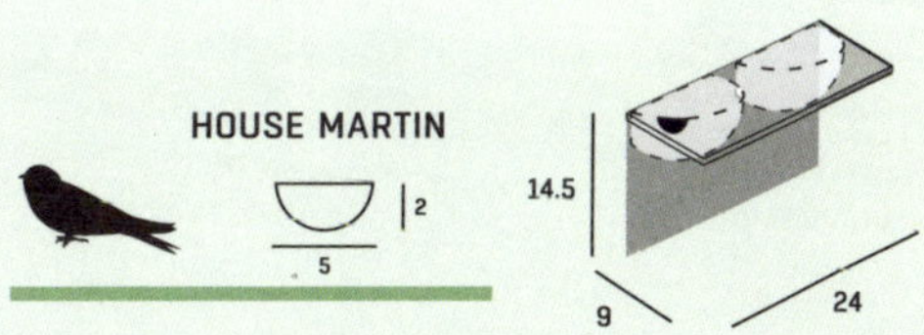

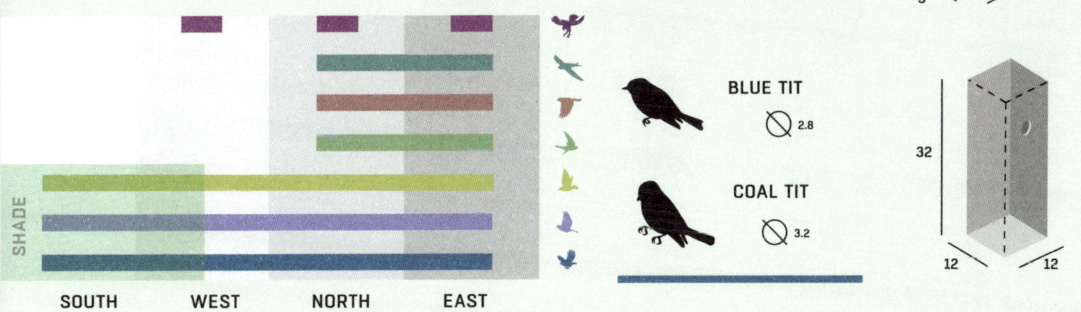

Triodosbank

Driebergen, RAU Architecten, 2019, NL

The Triodos Bank completed its new headquarters at the Reehorst Estate in 2019. The estate is part of the Nature Network Netherlands (NNN). The premise of the new building was to improve the national ecological network. The existing nature and natural elements with monumental and cultural-historical value, such as tree groves and sightlines, have been preserved as much as possible. The parts that did have to be removed have been compensated by creating new nature. This not only improves the quality of the NNN, but also extends it by more than 2.5 hectares. Thus, the NNN area south of the A12 motorway is connected via De Reehorst to the NNN area on the other side of the estate.

The building stands in a tree-enclosed space and a distance of ten 10 metres has been kept from the trees on site. The height of the building has also been restricted to be below the treetops. The design consists of several volumes rising in height, each with a green roof, from an intensive herb roof to an extensive moss sedum roof. To prevent birds from flying into the windows, overhangs have been realized that cast shadows on the glass. During construction, conservation measures were taken in accordance with BREAAM, trees were protected, the breeding season was taken into account, and disturbance by artificial light was avoided.

Design of the Reehorst Estate.
Left: The building has different green roofs, from extensive to intensive / Rainwater is stored in ponds present on the estate. In this way, water is available for plants and animals even in times of drought / One of the beeches that was already there, around which the building was formed / The building is lower than the treetops, so it does not disrupt bat flight paths.

Building & Bats

There are 1462 species of bats worldwide. This means that more than 20 per cent of all mammal species are bats. Consequently, there is great variation in behaviour and distribution, partly because bats (as the only species of mammals) can fly. In north-western Europe, all bats are insectivorous. Around 50 different species occur across Europe.

European bats can be broadly divided by their behaviour into two groups: arboreal bats and bats that prefer a stony environment, such as a cave or a building. And a number of species use both types of roosts, or use one or the other depending on the season. In the Netherlands, the common pipistrelle bat is the most common building-bound bat species and, like the serotine bat and the rarer pond bat, truly relies on buildings. Some more common species can sometimes be found in buildings but still prefer trees, such as noctule bat and Daubenton's bat. Less common, but also living in buildings, is the parti-coloured bat.

The Building as a Roost

The conditions for settlement in a building are the same for most species, although species differ in size. As a result, some species need a slightly larger access space to the roost than others. What all species have in common is a preference for cavities and crevices. A building actually provides the same function as natural crevices and cavities in rocks and caves. The main reason for choosing such a stone dwelling is that it is a durable and safe shelter with fairly constant climatic conditions in terms of humidity and temperature. In particular, buildings constructed from stone have this advantage because of its thermal properties: stone can absorb and retain heat well and therefore does not cool down as much during the night as other materials, such as wood. In addition, stone can provide insulation, including against cold from outside. And stone has the advantage that it usually has a rough surface for bats to hang on.

This roost then has to be close to foraging areas, as a long flight distance between the area where food is available and the permanent roost is not energetically rewarding. Ideally, therefore, a roost should be right next to an area with sufficient greenery and water to forage for insects and to drink.

One advantage of using a building as a roost is its higher temperature compared to the surroundings. Firstly, this is advantageous for overwintering, when bats hibernate to survive the cold months when food is almost non-existent. In addition, warmth is important in spring for pregnant or lactating females: the less heat that needs to be generated from fat burning, the better chance of survival for themselves and the

Long-eared bats in an attic.

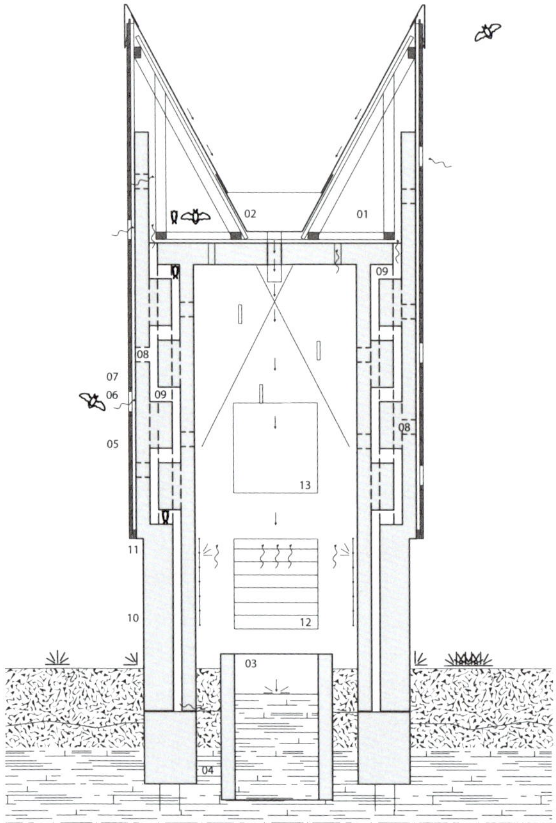

01. ATTIC / 02. GUTTER / 03. RAINWATER COLLECTION PIT / 04. GROUNDWATER 05. WOODEN CLADDING / 06. OPENINGS: W=22 MM / 07. AIR CAVITY / 08. OPENING BUTT JOINTS: W=22 MM/ 09. CAVITY LABYRINTH IN MASONRY/ 10. SMOOTH MASONRY 11. OVERHANG (ANTI-MICE) / 12. HEATING / 13. INSPECTION HATCH

The brick facades of these pond bat towers have a maze-like system of passages where the bats can look for a shelter that suits them at any particular time. The pond bat prefers relatively warm and moist spaces. Rain water collected in a barrel provides high atmospheric humidity. The tower is a research project with sensors that monitor climatic conditions inside. On the roof, in the gutters and on cantilevered bricks mosses and small plants can grow. (Pond bat towers, Amsterdam, Ruimtelab, Batweter, 2021, NL)

young. During the maternity period, bats are vulnerable and this time is crucial for the survival of the species. Finally, just as a tree cavity does for the other group of bats, the building provides protection from weather conditions such as wind and precipitation. Buildings therefore offer an opportunity to minimize energy consumption for the sake of survival in cold periods. Especially somewhat older buildings that have (leaked) heat in the cavity, have a heated space due to installations with radiation into the wall, and also buildings with draught-free attics and roofs offer this advantage. Besides temperature, the humidity balance is important because bats are prone to dehydration, partly due to their large wing area in relation to their body size. Bats therefore need a draught-free roost; so a cavity wall or bat box with too much airflow is not suitable. In winter, an environment with high humidity is preferred, as is the case in many forts, ice cellars and bunkers. Several species also use a residential building for hibernation, provided it meets the species' requirements.

Because of the sensitivity to indoor climate, there should be multiple options for roosts in a building, facing different wind directions, each with a different amount of sunshine

Common pipistrelle / Common long-eared bat / Daubenton's bat.

per day. The demand for variation is evidenced by the behaviour of bats in summer: when temperatures are too high, bats move to a northern facade, for example, while in spring a southern facade can be used (which will in turn be too hot in summer). Ideally, therefore, a roosting place is linked, so bats have many square metres at their disposal to crawl into the wall and turn a corner to find the best temperature and humidity at any given time. A provision of multiple roosts with different microclimates can greatly increase the survival rate of bats. This principle is the same for spaces under roofs and in attics, under bridges and in other types of buildings. In other words, bats move house frequently and need a network of roosts in different buildings, always looking for the optimal spot.

Water in the surrounding area is important: buildings are used especially if they are not too far away from fresh water. Water features should be dark, and thus not lit from a building or other light source. As one of the exceptions, a species like the common pipistrelle is less sensitive to light and does hunt for insects in bright spots in outdoor areas. Rows of trees near buildings can contribute to a flight path and provide wind cover, so bats can start foraging directly from the building. With a large green roof, blossom-bearing trees can also be used (plum, cherry) or shrubs such as raspberry or blackcurrant. Roof gardens or facade greenery with flowering plants can be attractive to insects and thus contribute to food for bats. Species suitable for this are yarrow, vervain, catnip or garden plants such as lavender. Native plants are important because of their attraction to the insects that bats hunt. Water lily or loosestrife can be used around or in ponds. If bat accommodation is made in a (blind) wall, facade vegetation should be kept away from this entrance. Bats cannot reach an entrance opening through planting and require an open approach route for this. Therefore, keep the opening clear of vegetation for about one metre.
It is important for bats that lighting is also limited or absent on and around the building. Illumination of the building (offices, churches, bridges are often illuminated with spotlights), bright gallery lights and garden lights left on all night are all negative for nocturnal animals such as bats. Lights with motion detectors will cause bats to avoid the area around the building. If lighting is absolutely necessary, lamps that do not cause stray light can be used, in a low level of lux from the lowest possible height, with the light falling only on the path.

Food

In north-western Europe, all bats are insectivores. They feed on mosquitoes, midges, lacewings, flies, mayflies, caddisflies, moths, micros and beetles, among others. The hunting technique and therefore diet varies between bat species, but all bats must also drink and need fresh water to do so.

Food is found on, in and above the water (Daubenton's bat and pond bat primarily hunt very low above the water) and in the air around vegetation (trees, shrubs and herbs). Some bats can also pick insects from grassland or leaves. The supply of food is leading in this regard; bats forage where the insects are present, thus visiting several places during the night. There are three main times when food is particularly important: for females during lactation, for males during mating season and for all species in autumn. In autumn, bats need to build up a fat reserve to survive hibernation without food.

Several Roosts

Bats have a somewhat unusual reproductive cycle. This also involves different roosts: mating roost, maternity roost, summer roost and winter roost. Mating takes place in autumn for most species. Building-dwelling species generally also use the building for this. A mating roost is often strategically located on the route between the maternity roost and the winter roost, or for some species near the winter roost, so that a male can attract females. These sites are reused annually, although there is probably also a network of multiple mating roosts per individual. Mating may also take place in the winter roost. This strategy varies between bat species, and it is likely that species use multiple strategies.

Females mate with multiple males. However, fertilization does not take place immediately. The female stores the seed over the winter and does not fertilize herself until spring, when the species has formed maternity colonies and the females seek out a large roost together: the maternity roost. Pregnancy lasts several weeks. The main advantage of this method is that the females can choose the optimal time for fertilization and embryo development so that birth coincides with the time when there is sufficient warmth and food in spring. The maternity roost can also be inhabited by females that are not yet sexually mature and by older females that no longer mate. It is a social structure in which animals support each other. Maternity roosts can consist of dozens of animals to many hundreds, depending on local possibilities such as the size of the roost and the distance to and presence of sufficient food.

Bats generally only give birth to one pup, sometimes two, a year. This makes bat reproduction vulnerable. And because a maternity colony sits together during this phase, disturbing such a roost is very risky. It is a delicate time: the mothers have to leave the colony for a while to hunt for food and return to suckle the pup. Sufficient food therefore has to be available within a short distance. The suckling period lasts for several weeks until the young are fledging and start hunting with the group. After this, the maternity group breaks up again. Every year, the maternity group returns. Maternity roosts are therefore very important: they must be large, stable, undisturbed and available every year so that no energy is lost looking for a new roost.

A summer roost is usually a smaller place, used by males that are solitary or gather in small groups during the maternity period or by females that are not pregnant and are

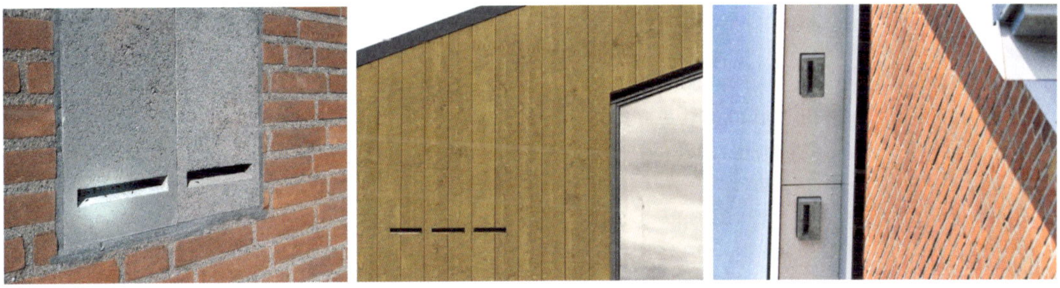

Built-in boxes for bats: in the brickwork, behind the facade or in the eaves.

not part of a maternity colony. During the summer, several roosts may be used, which is why a network of roosts is important.
Winter roosts are often different places from summer, maternity and mating roosts. Like maternity roosts, winter roosts are extremely vulnerable because bats go into deep torpor (hibernation) during this period in these roosts. At that time, the animals are not mobile and waking up takes time and energy. That energy is precisely what the animals need to conserve to use their fat reserves to get through the winter. A winter roost is in use for several months: many species hibernate for about five months. However, a winter roost can be inspected and used as early as autumn, also as a mating roost. Bats may well wake up briefly in winter time to fly a short distance or search for some water, only to go back into deep sleep, with the frequency in breathing and heart rate and metabolism greatly reduced. Disturbance of a winter roost should therefore be avoided at all times, as it greatly affects the survival rate of bats.

Bats may use multiple buildings because of varying climatic conditions throughout the year, but also because there are different requirements for each type of roost. Apart from this change due to different uses, bats also often move to avoid parasites. The entire network is therefore important, as bats rely on a variety of roosts. In consultation with an expert, it is useful to map out the species of bats and types of roosts already present in the area. Based on the species and functions already present, it can be determined which types of roosts can be realized in new buildings. Facilities should preferably be placed facing several wind directions and, if this is not possible on one building, spread over several buildings. A variation in size of the boxes is best; from a small mating roost to a very large maternity roost of several square metres in size built up in a number of layers, or where the bats have access to an entire cavity wall.

Practical Application for Roosts in Buildings

All built in features, such as nest boxes, come at the expense of the regular insulation layer. A higher-quality piece of insulation must therefore be made at the back to maintain the desired insulation value and prevent a thermal bridge. Furthermore, for all roosts, it is essential that no solvents are released. So, do not use treated or painted wood.
All types of roosts are needed. It is therefore good to vary what is installed in or onto a building. The most critical roosts are winter and maternity roosts, while somewhat lighter requirements apply to summer and mating roosts. Mating roosts need not be very large and can be easily installed. Mating roosts are also possible in bat boxes

and proven effective for many species (but not all). Summer roosts are similar to mating roosts: these do not need to be very large, but as small groups of bats may be involved here, it is therefore preferable to have them be somewhat larger.

Maternity roosts are extremely difficult to create. For most species, there is insufficient information available on how to make them effective. If possible, it is therefore best to provide an entire cavity wall in a place that does not cool down too much and preferably has some residual heat from the building. Realizing a roost near an existing maternity colony is most likely to succeed. Always consult with experts to explore possibilities in detail.

Winter roosts may be even more difficult to create, as they require considerable heat buffering and high humidity. It is possible to create an underground roost in consultation with an expert, in which case monitoring for effectiveness is important because the conditions are so critical. Sometimes high-rise buildings in a city are used as so-called mass winter roosts, where very large groups of bats roost together. The reason is that such places have a lot of available volume and surface area, good heat buffering and the place remains frost-free. And such a place cannot therefore be replaced with a built-in box, which requires customization in the new building and a long lead time with monitoring afterwards.

It applies to all functions that a bat box cannot easily be too large. A large surface area and several layers in depth are always preferred. The indoor temperature in a bat roost should be between 5 and 40 degrees Celsius, in a maternity roost at least 25 degrees Celsius.

The access opening to the different roosts must be appropriate, in other words not too small (the size of the skull and whether a female is pregnant are normative for this) and also safe, so not too large. With too large an opening, birds will enter or, if the space is even larger, other predators. An entrance to the cavity or a built-in bat box should therefore be between 15 and 20 mm in height. Less than 12 mm is too small; not even the smallest species can get through that. The width of the gap can vary between 50 mm and 50 cm to a metre. This could be an open butt joint, a small gap under a windowsill with access to the cavity, a masonry ventilation grille, or a custom-made access in the wall to a space behind it. With a gap height of 25 mm or more, the likelihood of a bird crawling in is too high and the box will not be used by bats. When making multiple roosts, a single access of 25 mm is okay, though, to get some variation for the larger bats and pregnant ones.

There should be a usable landing site in front of the entrance: there should be no slippery material at the entrance opening as a bat will not have a grip. So below the entrance opening there needs to be a vertical surface, about 30 cm high and rough enough for a bat to land on and crawl inside.

The entrance opening may not be lit by artificial light: so no lamps. This has everything to do with safety from predators. There must be an obstacle-free flight space of several metres from the roost to stay out of reach of predators. Usually, a 5-metre radius is used for this in which no trees or flagpoles and the like can stand. It is known that domestic cats can snatch bats out of the air if the exit opening of bats is within their reach because, for example, there is an extension next to the building and the domestic cat has climbed onto that roof.

Inside the building or the created space, there should be sufficient shelter from cold, overheating, dehydration (drafts) and precipitation. And from disturbance by people

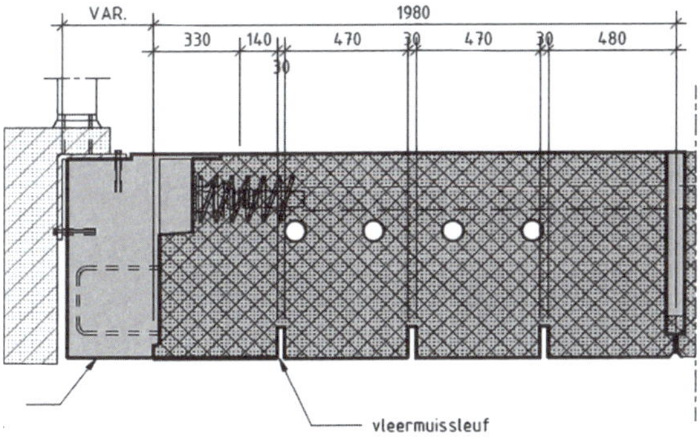

The 'scratches', trenches about 6 cm deep in the underside of the bridge deck are intended as spaces where nature can obtain a foothold. Common pipistrelles, for example may use them to sleep and find shelter. (Kattenbrug, Groningen, Korth Tielens Architects, DS landschapsarchitecten, 2023, NL)

(presence, lighting) and predators, in the case of an open (church) attic or underground roost.

In the roost itself, the bat needs material to hang from with its nails. So, a smooth wall such as a metal one will not do. Stone, rough or roughened (wood) concrete and wood are fine. Bats can also roost under roof tiles, provided it does not get too hot in summer. Just access from the gutter is sufficient, or from the end wall via the ridge. No smooth insulation material or vapour barrier film should be present under the roof. It is important that vapour-permeable film is not made of frayed material; the threads that can come loose entangle the animals and make a roost unsuitable and even dangerous.

A specially constructed roost offers the best guarantee of a successful stay.

But 'ordinary' building parts can also be suitable. At least they were for a long time in traditionally constructed (stone) buildings. An intermediate cavity that is accessible can work fine if the cavity has at least 3 centimetres of space and does not have a smooth finish on the inside. An open expansion joint can provide a long crevice-shaped space for bats to roost, if it is deep enough and not too wide because of birds that might otherwise enter the roost and thus chase the bats away.

Bats can also roost behind facade panelling or fascia boards, provided that sufficient square metres are available. The entrance should be at least 15 mm for smaller species to a maximum of 25 mm for larger species. Once inside, there can be a space that is wider, in fact this is desirable so that bats have room to groom themselves. To optimize the space behind the entrance, multiple layers (in depth) can be made,

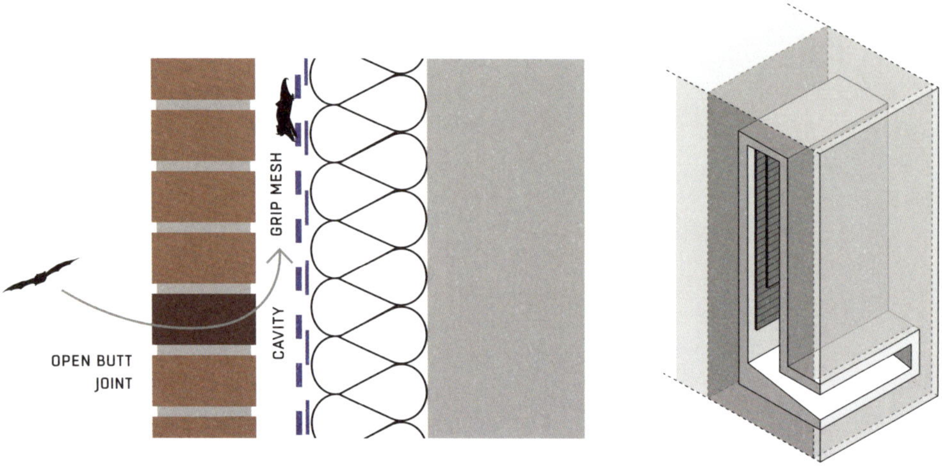

Left: The air cavity still proves to be the best dwelling place for a bat. Right: Inner dimensions of a multi-layered built-in box: bespoke, in consultation with an ecologist (at least 12 mm between the slats, at most 35 mm; the entrance should not be larger than 25 mm to prevent bird using the box). The larger the box and the more layers, the better. Material: rough surface for grip; concrete or wood and concrete mixture is the most sustainable material.

and horizontal slats that stagger (align left one time, right the next) are also used to create multiple zones.

Under eaves and in a building's overhang, bats can find a place to roost just like behind facade panelling and fascia boards. Customization is possible here when constructing new buildings, although it is not proven effective for all species. An entrance opening is best made against the wall, so bats can land on this rough surface and then crawl inside. With a large facility, it is necessary to make several openings, including one for ventilation, but not too many, because of the risk of draughts.

If insulation material is used in new buildings, it is important that there is roughness in the air cavity (of at least 30 mm) where the bat can hang by its nails and crawl. To this end, a smooth insulation board can be roughened with cement or a form-fitting mesh can be placed over it. This is called grip netting (mesh size between 3-10 mm), intended to give bats grip. However, breathable material such as wood, stone and wood concrete works best. Roughened material such as plastic or metal will not work, and material with fibres that can come loose should always be avoided.

The heights for built-in facilities and entrance openings can vary, from a minimum of 4 metres in height to around 25 metres for the zone where most bats will roost, ranging up to 50 metres in height, with some species, such as the parti-coloured bat, appearing to prefer the altitude. However, sometimes tall buildings are also used as mass winter quarters by, for example, pipistrelles. Most successful are facilities that hanging under a window sill, overhang or gutter, or some ornamental edge that sticks out a little. These are places that bats find the quickest. Experts say that this is more important than an exact height.

Many species use low-rise buildings, so under 15 metres. Corner houses and detached houses with a ridge top are often useful for many species (including birds), as this gives bats access to a large suface of open cavity. Bats and birds will not share a roost; it does happen that there are two species of bats in one roost.

Maintenance

In principle, bat boxes require no maintenance. Bat boxes are designed so that the bottom plate is slanted and excrement does not remain in the box, but washes away. The material often consists of wood concrete, or it is an accessible cavity. Bats do not gnaw or take nesting material inside, so cleaning is not necessary. However, spiders may have made a web in the box, causing a bat to be less likely to use the box; therefore, a check every three years is recommended to remove the webs. Ideally, this could be combined with painting work on a property, when facilities are in place anyway, making maintenance and inspection a small effort. Of course, this can only be done when the box is not in use.

Renovation Challenge

Building-dwelling bats are currently at high risk, due to the rate at which traditional roosts are disappearing. On the one hand, this is due to demolition: older buildings are given a different function and the new buildings no longer have heat leaks and are built in a different way, virtually eliminating cavities and crevices. On the other hand, older buildings are being insulated. This post-isolation is proceeding at a very fast pace. Post-insulation not only causes roosts to disappear, but also kills many animals. They are trapped and cannot get out of the space, or die from contact with the material and fumes of the insulation. Bats often cannot escape in time, especially during a cold period. In a colder period, the animals are in deep torpor, during which they have a very low heart rate. They only manage to fly or crawl away after a period of warming up. And if an animal escapes the post-insulation, a new roost must then be found nearby. When entire residential areas are post-insulated, it is obvious that there are not enough of them left, if no measures are taken. This is where climate and biodiversity meet: post-insulation is desirable from a climate objective perspective, but not at the expense of biodiversity loss. Nature-inclusive building therefore has to become the norm so that both major challenges can be addressed simultaneously, also in the urban area.

Nature-exclusive Design

Not all species of animals and plants are welcome on the building. Thus, it is sometimes necessary to design nature-exclusively to keep out these unwanted guests.

Even if we find some animals and plants undesirable, terms like 'pests' and 'weeds' should not be used. These are not objective observations or designations of a living species. They are opinions, which may indeed differ depending on the context. A butterfly-bush is usually a desired plant, but never if it grows from a quay wall or if this species spreads invasively through a nature area. And house mosquitoes are food for bats, birds, dragonflies and beetles (and the larvae also for fish), but we humans don't appreciate them much. So, there are all kinds of plants and animals that we perceive as troublesome, and there are many invasive species that we would rather not invite into our habitat. In many ways, this is the opposite of nature-inclusive measures. Where establishment conditions are optimized for wanted species, they are omitted or frustrated for unwanted ones. The main three conditions are food, safety with a place to stay, and reproduction with nesting opportunities. To ensure that a particular species will not be present in and around a house, one or more of these factors can be removed. For instance, the litter we leave on our streets, in particular, is a welcome food source for many species for which we do not want to build nature-inclusively. No street litter? Then there will also be much less nuisance from rats, gulls and feral pigeons.

In the urban area, there is one 'pest' that stands out in terms of notoriety: the feral pigeon. A species that is very opportunistic: wherever people leave food behind, intentionally or unintentionally, you can find this species in the urban area. Frequently used sites are characterized by lots of faeces, and that aspect often causes the most nuisance. To prevent feral pigeons from nesting, recesses and flat ledges in buildings should be avoided in the design. To avoid unsightly bird spikes on a windowsill, they can also be designed at an angle that prevents birds from resting on them. Bird spikes on new buildings are basically a sign of poor design.

After the feral pigeon, the brown rat is perhaps the second most unwelcome species in the city. This species can carry diseases such as Weil's disease and therefore a large concentration of rats is potentially dangerous to humans. Again, food supply is particularly

The brown rat feels at home in the city.

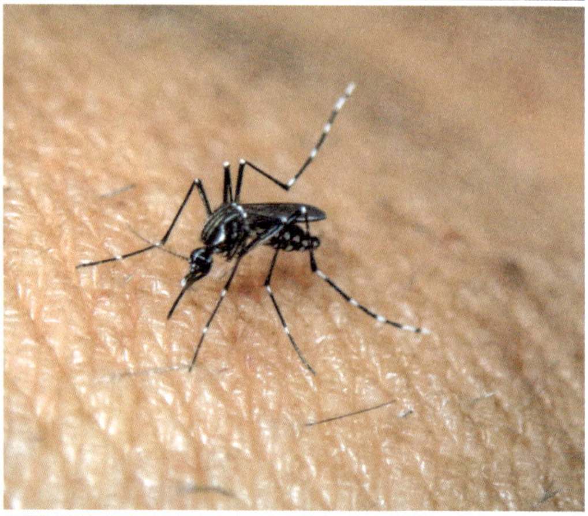

determinant, which can be resolved by putting litter in bins that have lids. They can be prevented from making a burrow under a building by ensuring that there is no accessible space directly under the foundation, while taking care that ventilation does remain intact.

To prevent mosquito nuisance, it is important to avoid stagnant water that is shallow and heats up quickly. For instance, in places such as gutters, water butts and plant pots or bowls on a roof terrace. When designing buildings and green roofs, it is essential to make sure that the water collection is sealed. This will prevent mosquitoes from laying their eggs there, from which larvae would then develop into adult mosquitoes. Especially with the rise of diseases like West Nile virus that mosquitoes can transmit, this is an important area of concern now and in the future.

Then there are the species that can cause nuisance inside our homes, such as the house mouse, spiders or grey silverfish. Species that only need a small space in the house and that not everyone is happy with. Oftentimes, it is the food, warmth, humidity and the shelter provided by the house that determines the presence of a species.

As for plants, the planting of invasive exotics and allergens on a green roof, green facade or around a house should be avoided. Sometimes species come with the soil, therefore, at realization, it should be known for sure where a consignment of soil comes from, to prevent spreading. When planting greenery, care should be taken not to purchase species that are undesirable; this can be avoided from the design stage by using native material. When maintaining this greenery, it is very important to actively remove invasive exotic plant species, such as Japanese knotweed (which proliferates very quickly) and ragweed (a plant that can cause hay fever), when they first appear in the planting. If you remove these plants, the plant material and soil should not be disposed of with green waste, but with residual waste.

Finally, in situations where plants of any kind are undesirable in the design, it is essential to ensure that substrate cannot accumulate and that moisture and light are not present. Only when these basic conditions are removed can it be guaranteed that the area remains free of flora that is not wanted, and thus kept nature-exclusive.

European herring gulls foraging on waste / Common ragweed / Asian tiger mosquito / Domestic animals such as the domestic cat are among the most threatening predators for many bats, birds and small mammals.

5

Our countryside is increasingly looking like an admittedly green, but still industrial desert. For the greatest diversity of life, you now have to be near the cities. In fact, to teach people about biodiversity and natural cycles, you don't need to go to Brazil or Australia either. I can stand at a Rotterdam roadside and tell a delightful story about plants that feed insects, which then feed songbirds and eventually sparrow hawks and peregrine falcons.

JELLE REUMER

Green Facades and Roofs

The connection between the adjacent outdoor space and the building is essential for the success of nature-inclusive measures. Many species that use the building also need a suitable environment outside the building. Therefore, it is good to provide a transition zone between the building and its surroundings. This zone forms a gradual transition and thus provides a diversity of habitats for plants and animals. Greening the facade, including the outdoor spaces located on the facade, such as terraces and balconies, is the most appropriate means to this end.

There are different systems for green facades, depending on the growth habit and position of the planting: growing roots in the open ground at the foot of the building, in green systems mounted on the facade or directly in the facade material.

For plants climbing up from the open ground along the facade, a distinction can be made between self-attachers, creepers and vines/support-climbers. Self-attachers, such as ivy and Virginia creeper, adhere directly to the outer leaf, while creepers such as honeysuckle and wisteria wind themselves around previously installed vertical cables. Support-climbers and vines seek foothold on horizontal elements, with vines such as traveller's joy and passionflower using their tendrils, while support-climbers such as firethorn and jasmine lean on horizontal elements such as cables.
Self-attachers have a bad name because the roots are said to damage masonry and woodwork. Ivy and creeper in particular, seek out cracks and holes to attach themselves to the structure behind. Where lime-rich mortar has been applied, the pointing can be damaged, which can be prevented with modern concrete mortar. Roots can also creep behind the woodwork, causing damage. Proper detailing combined with maintenance of climbing plants can prevent this.
Another approach is to install a separate wooden or steel outer cavity leaf to which the plants can cling and which is allowed to get damaged. In this case, however, it is important to protect the underlying structure, especially the insulation, with root-resistant canvas.

If there is no room to grow plants from the open ground against the facade, an auxiliary structure containing substrate and water supply is required. An example is the 'living wall' system, which consists of cassettes or mats with substrate and planting. A variant of this is a wall consisting of stones in a gabion system with an irrigation system.

L'Oasis d'Aboukir, Paris (Patrick Blanc, 2013).

There are also examples of facades with containers attached to them These relatively heavy containers must be attached to the supporting structure behind the facade with anchors. For non-insulated facades, such as parking garages, this is easier than for insulated facades where thermal bridges must be avoided. Unlike 'living walls', which form a continuous system, these wall-mounted containers do not need to be interconnected.
An advantage of systems added to the facade is that planting can grow at great heights and provide an artificial but rich green environment in dense inner cities. However, this variant is less robust than that in which the planting grows from the open ground, as the planting is dependent on the technology. If the technology fails, the plants may die.

A third variant is that in which the planting roots directly into the facade material, without using a special facade structure. This growth can be facilitated by enlarging the attachment surface of the facade material itself. For example, by adding holes, ridges and grooves, or by using porous material. Simpler but more vulnerable is the application of lava rock, suitable for garden walls but not for structural masonry.
Wall plants, ferns and mosses make use of a minimal amount of substrate that has accumulated over time in crevices and joints and the rainwater seeping down the wall. Masonry with lime-rich mortar combined with moisture coming through the wall from behind, as in retaining walls and quay walls, provides a suitable habitat for mosses and wall plants. This type of planting has adapted to fluctuations in moisture and can therefore function without special water systems or nutrient inputs.

Plant Containers
Plant containers are often used for plants and trees on balconies and terraces. The containers come in many different sizes and shapes, ranging from tubes 30 cm in diameter to 2-metre-high containers for trees. Elongated planters, for example along the edges of roof terraces, can be incorporated into the construction and architecture as a structural component. Of course, if no structural plant containers are fitted, there is always room for a range of larger and smaller pots, moveable or not.
These containers and the larger pots have a substrate with a water retention layer underneath. The greenery depends on water and nutrients, making an artificial irrigation system a prerequisite. To prevent the containers from becoming too heavy during heavy rainfall, an overflow is required.
In new construction, it is a choice to invest in a heavier structure. Especially when choosing trees in containers on balconies, this is relevant. For instance, when placed at the edge of cantilevered outdoor spaces, an extra heavy support structure is needed.

It is not yet standard in new buildings, but there is every reason to combine facade greenery with animal housing such as bird nest boxes and insect accommodations. For the latter, it is important that the vegetation also provides food for insects. This could be a selection of nectar plants that flower at different times of the year, but common ivy also provides food for bumblebees and bees in late summer and subsequently produces berries for some birds. And garden birds such as the blackbird like to nest in a green

A facade for various types of climbing plants, with a sealed concrete exterior cavity leaf without gaps and holes. The window frames prevent plants from growing in front of the glass. (Residential building, Het Funen, Amsterdam, Geurst & Schulze, 2007, NL)

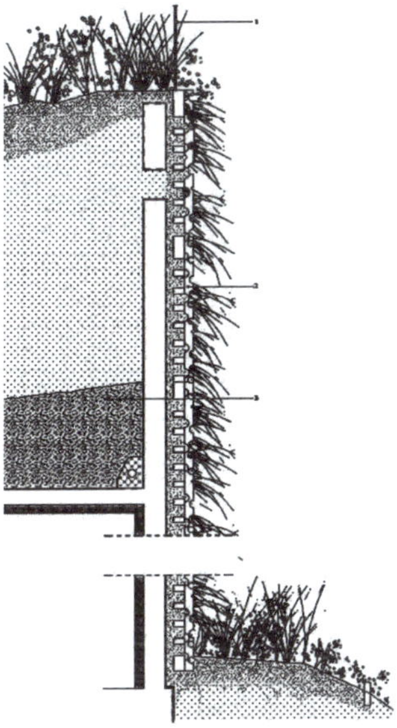

At the base of the building, 390 m² of the facade has a pattern of holes. Through the interconnected openings, the substrate in the wall is connected to the soil around the building and that of the roof gardens. This creates equal conditions and because the substrate is inside the wall, it is less susceptible to drying out. (Head office AP-HP hôpitaux, Paris, ChartierDalix, 2022, FR)

At this Ricola company warehouse, water runs from the roof along the concrete facade, enough for algae and small mosses to grow. When there is an abundance of water, a low-tech solution can be sufficient. (Ricola Europe, Mulhouse, Herzog&deMeuron, 1993, CH)

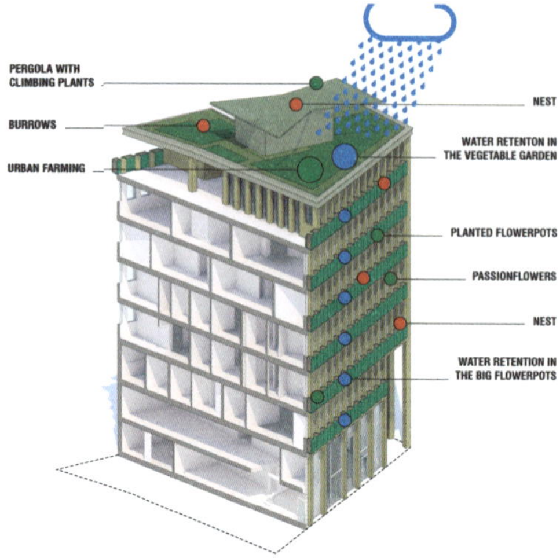

The greenery in the 290 plant containers, an average of 14 per dwelling, creates a green enclave in this stony part of Paris. (Edison Lite, Paris, Manuelle Gautrand Architecture, Bureau Bas Smets, 2020, FR)

facade, because of its shelter and safe height. When placing and maintaining nest boxes, make sure they do not overgrow with the greenery, otherwise the facilities will no longer work.

Green Roofs

Until recently, the flat roof was nothing more than a passive building component, a place for technical equipment, finished with cheap materials. In recent years, the roof has been rediscovered and put to use for energy generation, as a collective outdoor space, for growing food, as water storage and as a biotope for plants and animals. Experiments with new roof systems are therefore in full swing. In doing so, different 'colours' can be distinguished on the basis of primary function; green (primary natural value), blue (water storage), purple (food production), yellow (solar energy generation), red (residential space for people) and brown (sparsely vegetated and stony for nature). Looking at the management and complexity of vegetation, a distinction is also made between extensive roofs (limited maintenance, less complex vegetation, relatively thin substrate package) and intensive roofs (more complex vegetation and maintenance, thicker substrate layer), also called biodiversity roofs. The ecosystem services provided by a green roof include insulation, attenuation of warming through shading and evaporation, and savings in water runoff at ground level.

Roofs typically have a high wind load and as there is a lack of shadow, they are a relatively dry environment. For this reason, the roof was designed as a dune landscape with associated vegetation that can withstand wind and periods of drought.

Over time, the facades of this residential building, equipped with nest boxes and insect bricks, will become overgrown. Openings in the horizontally extended facade elements allow vegetation to grow upwards from the full soil along the facade. (Residential building Groenmarkt, Amsterdam, Ronald Janssen architecten, Bastiaan Jongerius architecten, Buro Harro, 2022, NL)

The increased claim on the roof may lead to competition. The choice for an ecological green roof may then lose out to other options. A clever combination of functions may provide a solution. For example, a 'yellow' energy roof with solar panels can be nicely combined with a green roof. A roof where the greenery is also partly used as a roof terrace can be designed to have a frequently visited part and a part where there is no access. In this way, recreational use and ecological value can still go hand in hand. The primary function of food-producing roofs is not always aligned with providing habitat for insects and birds, but with extensive methods, a combination is indeed possible.

There are three aspects in which roof gardens differ fundamentally from ground-level gardens. The first is the wind load. This is greater at height than at ground level, which affects vegetation. Not all planting can cope with high winds, and trees and

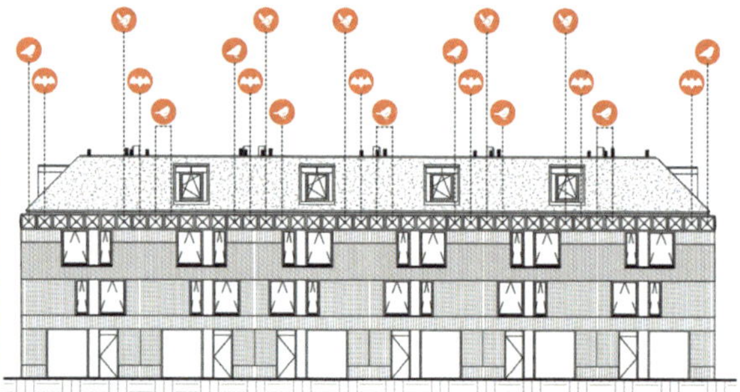

Within the walls of the Dobbelmann monastery, two completely wooden residential buildings and a gatehouse enclose a communal garden. The application of wood, pitched green roofs and recycled materials in the gatehouse help minimize the environmental impact. Together with an ecologist, an inventory was made of what was already there in terms of city flora and fauna and what nature-inclusive measures could be taken. The result is a roof edge ornamented with 127 nest boxes for birds and bats. The design is an interpretation of the monumental facades of the former monastery. (Hortus Ludi, Nijmegen, Studio Architectuur MAKEN, 2023, NL)

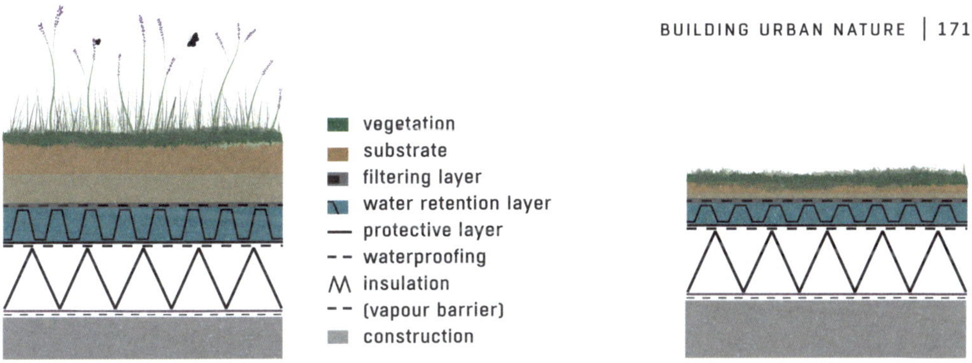

Left: Intensive green roof, with a thick layer of substrate, herbs, shrubs or even trees, requires more maintenance
Right: Extensive green roof, with a thin layer of substrate and low planting; requires little maintenance.

Broadly speaking, minimum thickness is suitable for sedum, thicker for herbs, even thicker for shrubs and the thickest package is also suitable for trees. Extensive, in this case with not very diverse vegetation, is 4-7 cm thick, while an intensive roof (with trees and shrubs) requires (possibly locally) 80-120 cm thickness. A natural roof with relief can also be achieved with 20-40 cm of substrate thickness. Locally, the weight on a roof can often be higher if there is a load-bearing structure underneath.

larger shrubs will need to be anchored. The sun load is also usually greater due to the lack of shading from trees and adjacent buildings. The third aspect is drought, partly caused by wind and lack of shade, but also by the lack of groundwater. Almost without exception, green roofs have to be artificially irrigated during dry periods.

Construction

As with the facade, nature-inclusive green roof facilities are located outside the building structure. On the substructure and insulation are the waterproofing membrane and a root barrier fabric with a water drainage layer on top, usually consisting of plastic cassettes with a channel system, which drains the excess rainwater, delayed by the labyrinth-like structure, into the rainwater system. Optionally, the bottom of the drainage layer can consist of a section where the water can be retained. The thickness of this so-called retention layer can be as much as 10 centimetres, but is of course highly dependent on the additional load allowed. The advantage of such a retention layer is not only that it improves the hydrological performance of the roof by keeping the substrate layer slightly moist, but also that it reduces the burden on the municipal sewage system. A filter fabric is then placed on top of the drainage and retention layer. This is necessary to prevent the water drainage system from becoming clogged with substrate or growing roots. The vulnerability of a green roof system mainly lies in the fact that possible leaks are very difficult to detect and fix. Extra attention must therefore be paid to the waterproofing of the structure. Avoid moisture accumulation in the seams of the root barrier and waterproofing layers. In times of drought, plants seek moisture and can cause leaks with their roots in these very places. Nevertheless, after years of experience with green roofs, it can be concluded that the service life of the underlying roof is increased by a factor of two.

Finally, the substrate layer in which the plants can grow is installed on this technical substrate. Thickness and composition of the substrate mixture will depend on the construction of the roof, along with other requirements such as water absorption and desired plant species. Usually, the substrate layer consists of soil mixed with material that retains moisture longer and may or may not have additional nutrients. Lava rock or baked clay pellets can be used for this, or the soil can be mixed with moisture-absorbing material such as coconut fibre or vermiculite. It is also possible to omit these additives and apply a layer of 'regular' garden soil in which natural soil life can develop. However, this layer will then be thicker and extra care must be taken to prevent drying out.
For greater diversity, the roof can be divided into different substrate zones. Bare sand can provide nesting opportunities for insects and a habitat for plants that prefer nutrient-poor conditions. Calcareous sand can provide conditions for species that need this mineral. And a zone with a thick layer of leaf litter provides habitat for other species. Finally, it is important to prevent the substrate from becoming compressed and too compact due to treading, preventing rain from infiltrating.
It is possible to transplant soil from the surrounding area onto the roof: to do this, set aside a layer of excavated soil and place it on the roof after construction. It will then contain the seeds that were already naturally present, but soil life such as fungi and bacteria will also come along. This can create equivalent conditions for the planting already present around the project yet to be realized.

The layer in which plants or even trees grow is the vegetation layer. While it is theoretically possible to maintain a green roof without additional watering, in practice, especially given the increased extremes of drought, it is necessary to irrigate the plants during dry periods. This can be done manually, but it is more common to install an irrigation system, possibly computer-controlled and automated.

The thickness of a substrate layer can range from a few centimetres to more than a metre. For plant life, soil life and insects, a thick substrate layer is always better. It provides resilience in relation to moisture and nutrients, allows larger species of plants or even trees to grow and thus attracts higher biodiversity on the roof.
For existing buildings in particular, the structure is the determining factor. If the load-bearing capacity of a roof is limited, a thicker soil layer can be applied where the structure allows more load, such as in zones with columns and/or beams.

Green Roof
The main reason for choosing a green roof is that the plants provide a habitat for numerous organisms. Intensive green roofs such as an herb roof or a roof garden, with a substrate layer of more than 15 centimetres, provide a basis for a wide

A Polderdak, as applied in the patio of a student housing building in Amsterdam, can contribute to a pleasant and cool outdoor space. (Minervahaven, Amsterdam, Dakdokters, 2022, NL)

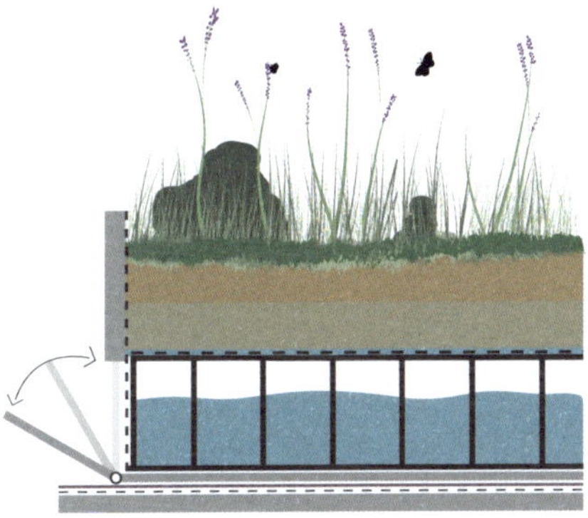

Left: vegetation, substrate, filtering layer, water retention layer, protective layer, waterproofing, insulation, construction, barrage / A Polderdak (Polder Roof) retains rainwater and provides irrigation for the roof garden from below. A remotely controlled barrage regulates the water level.

variety of plants. If the thickness exceeds 30 centimetres, shrubs can also be added. Moreover, the substrate layer itself can retain 50 to 80 per cent of rainwater. A thick package ensures that excess rainwater does not have to be drained off immediately, due to evaporation. A thicker package is suitable for a wide variety of wild bees, bumblebees and other insects that nest in the soil. Some bumblebees nest up to half a metre deep. Herb roofs and roof gardens do not only provide shelter but also food for micro-organisms, insects and thus numerous birds. Roofs are in many cases inaccessible to predators such as the domestic cat, so young birds are more likely to survive on a green roof where no people come.

A tree requires at least 60 but preferably 90 centimetres of substrate. Planting trees and shrubs on roofs adds value because of the shade, wind shelter and hiding places. Shrubs including berry-bearing and blossom-bearing species such as

The use of different types of substrates: parts with poor (calcareous) sand, parts with loamy sand, a part brown roof and some more nutrient-rich parts, encourages a varied vegetation. (Brown roof, Dusty Gedge, Londen, GB)

Utility roof, in this example a terrace in combination with a green roof / Solar panels produce more power when they are not too hot. Sedum and herb roofs contribute to a lower ambient temperature through evaporation from the underside and therefore have a beneficial effect on solar panel output.

Pitched roofs of up to 45 degrees can be fitted with vegetation. (Natuurlijk wonen, Westbroek, ORGA architect, 2022, NL)

hawthorn and wild cherry provide food for insects and birds. The advantage of shrubs is that they can often grow quite tall, but require less rooting space than trees.

Blue Roof

If water retention and relieving the sewage system is the primary function of the green roof, it is also referred to as a so-called 'polder roof'. In a relatively high retention layer, rainwater is stored and released to the sewage system in a delayed manner. A crucial part of the system is a movable valve placed in front of the rainwater drain. Thanks to sensors, this valve ensures that the roof retains as much rainwater as possible and only discharges it when possible or necessary due to an upcoming rainstorm.

There are also blue roofs constructed for other reasons. For instance, there are roofs intended to clean grey water through helophyte filters or roofs with ponds as part of the landscape plan. These ponds or marsh filters should then, like most garden ponds, be provided with a watertight bed. Such open water on the roof does run the risk of running dry in the summer period, when evaporation can be from a few millimetres to as much as a centimetre a day.

Brown Roof and Gravel Roofs

A special type of roof for biodiversity is the brown roof. Here, the substrate, which is drier and less nutrient-rich, consists of sand, gravel and rubble, possibly supplemented with dead tree trunks. A brown roof provides a biotope for pioneer species (species that are the first to settle on bare, sparse soil) and birds that have this type of terrain as their habitat. For example, the black redstart forages on such roofs and nests in this biotope.

The succession of different species and the development into a stable ecosystem can be simulated on such roofs, also known as 'nature roofs'. The aim of a nature roof is to create a sustainable and self-regulating roof adapted to local conditions. An initial start is made with mostly pioneer species. After a few years, successional vegetation will take over: the process of natural succession is given free rein here. Shrubs and later small trees can take their place in these gardens. The hallmark of a nature roof is that the plants that thrive best in the current conditions of the location grow there, along with all the species of animals this attracts.

Conventional gravel roofs, where the gravel acts as ballast, have been discovered by oystercatchers, the common tern and several species of gulls. These species breed on sandy or stony substrates. The natural biotope of beaches and dunes is disturbed by recreational visitors and the growing number of foxes. Urban roofs are a good and safe alternative, provided there is also some shelter in the form of a piece of sewer pipe or a pallet.

Yellow-green Roof

The use of solar panels combines very well with vegetation. Positioning the solar panels slightly further apart and on slightly higher legs creates an alternating microclimate (shaded, and semi-shaded, wind-protected) with space for different plants and shelter for birds.

Pile supports under the underwater bicycle parking are lined with structures in which mussels and small fish can thrive / Cages filled with shells provide a habitat for a variety of water plants and animals. (Bicycle parking, IJboulevard Amsterdam, VenhoevenCS architecture + urbanism, DS landschapsarchitecten, 2023, NL)

Auxiliary structures prevent dangerous situations at weak spots in the quays along Amsterdam's canals. These support structures are designed to allow nature to establish itself there temporarily.

Pitched Roofs
Pitched roofs can also be greened, depending on the degree of inclination. Up to about 15 degrees of inclination, the structure is similar to a flat roof. For steeper roofs, provisions should be made to prevent the substrate layer from slipping and washing away. Erosion can be prevented, for example, by placing barriers or ribs on the roof. The permissible thickness of the substrate layer can be considerable, depending on the size of such barriers.

Quays and Bridges
Connecting to the blue ecological structure, especially in water-rich cities, is also to be considered. The quays and banks, especially where the building's foot is in the water offer opportunities to facilitate nature. Dutch canals, but also canals in other north-western European cities, with their masonry quay walls, provide a biotope for ferns, mosses and wall plants. Older quays show irregularities and cracks that give wall plants a foothold. Moreover, the walls absorb moisture not only from the water below but also from rainwater that seeps through the walls from the street side. Traditional quay stone is relatively soft and water-absorbent and was built with lime-rich mortar until a hundred years ago. This somewhat softer mortar provides substrate for wall plants. The species that thrive here are thus native to rocky areas, are calcicolous and do well in moist environments.
Many canal quays in historical Dutch cities are in need of renovation. Loads from road traffic and subsidence caused by adjacent buildings make the walls unstable. The choice is often made to replace the masonry quay walls with a concrete retaining wall or steel sheet piling with a brick finish. Made with hard clinkers and impermeable concrete mortar, these exterior retaining walls are impermeable and therefore sterile and void of vegetation. In response to the disappearance of the typical biotope, experiments are underway that mimic the conditions of the old quay walls to provide a habitat for the characteristic quay vegetation to grow.

To enable plant growth, new construction methods are also being looked into. Water management plays a crucial role here. Traditional quay walls are not only damp on the underside just above the water line, but are also wet because water seeps through the wall from behind via small cracks in the masonry and pointing.
For instance, to create damp walls, openings are provided. Rainwater from the street can enter the cavity through openings under the capstone or special wall coverings. To increase the dampness of the cavity even higher up the wall, the cavity is filled with moisture-absorbing material. Applying lime-rich mortars in new quay walls is not desirable everywhere from a maintenance and lifespan point of view. However, grouting can be done with special mortars to create a lime-rich top layer.
To spare vegetation on existing traditional masonry walls, sections can be skipped during wall cleaning. Ligneous species should, however, be removed as they root deeper than wall plants and can therefore damage the grouting and wall.
Bridges, in particular, offer opportunities. A characteristic feature of a bridge is the underside of the bridge deck which, especially on fixed bridges, is suitable for birds and bats. The pylons and underwater structure provide opportunities for measures

Maintenance of the vegetation roof of the École des sciences et de la biodiversité. (ChartierDalix, 2014, FR)
Abseiling gardeners tend the balcony gardens of Bosco Verticale, Milan. (Stefano Boeri Architetti, 2014, IT)

In the city of Utrecht more than 300 bus shelters were covered with a total of 2000 m² of sedum roof. Because of the scale of this citywide project it is suited for monitoring and as a research project. (Green bus shelters, Utrecht, Municipality of Utrecht, 2021, NL)

to stimulate plant attachment and structures in which small fish can shelter and freshwater mussels can attach. Both as places to nest and live, not least because of their close proximity to food in the form of insects and small aquatic life.

Management and Maintenance of Green Facades and Roofs

It is true for all facilities that they also need to be managed. If time and money are not set aside for maintenance, it is debatable whether these facilities should be realized. The maintenance of a green facade and green roof is generally intensive. Plants are not in full soil and have no contact with groundwater, so the supply of water and nutrients has to be managed. Usually with an irrigation network and sometimes by adding nutrients to the water, especially for facade plants. For wall-mounted plants, maintenance is required to replenish any soil that has been washed away, to remove ligneous species that spontaneously start to grow between the plants, and refill of dead material is usually desired. If necessary, vents, windows and gutters can be cut free if plant growth is unwanted there. Because of the height, this often requires the use of equipment that allows landscapers to work safely. In extreme cases, it even requires landscapers to descend using climbing harnesses to maintain facade greenery. Maintenance on a green roof mainly requires control of water drainage and will otherwise need usual maintenance (at least if that is desired and natural succession is not pursued) as is done for a ground-level garden. If the roof also has a residential function, the customary safety precautions are necessary (fall protection). If the roof is only accessed for maintenance, a safety line will suffice.

TYPE A1: National Museum Oslo, Kleihues + Schuwerk, 2021, NO / **TYPE A2**: Restructuring Genderdal, Eindhoven, Buro Lubbers, 2013, NL / **TYPE B1**: MTV building, London, Biotecture, 2015, GB / **TYPE B2**: Building that grows, Montpellier, Maison Edouard François, 2000, FR / **TYPE B3**: Technical space, Malmö, Galeasens Gränd, SE / **TYPE C**: Main offices, AP-HP hôpitaux, Parijs, ChartierDalix, 2022, FR / Below: Retaining wall in the Griftpark in Utrecht with lime-rich joints and porous bricks.

Green Facade Typology

Green facades can be divided into three main types. Facades where the plants take root in the full soil; systems that are attached to the building as an external facade finish; and facades where the plants grow directly from the facade material.

The first type is characterized by planting that adheres directly to the facade (type A1). The planting, such as ivy and Virginia creeper, attaches to the uneven surfaces of the brick or protruding facade parts. Another type where the planting also grows out of the full soil are facades where the planting can attach to cables or a support structure in front of the facade (type A2).

Because there is not always space in densely built-up inner cities to grow plants from the ground in front of the facade, the living wall was developed (type B1). This is how landscape architect Patrick Blanc applied the Mur Vegetal to facades in Paris and numerous cities around the world. The system now has many variants involving cassettes with substrate and an irrigation system. To prevent over- or under-watering, software is used that adds more or less water based on the weather forecast. Nutrients are added to the water because the limited volume of substrate cannot produce its own nutrients.

A variation on this is the 'brown' living wall (type B2). Another type in this category are systems whereby planters are attached directly to the load-bearing wall (type B3). Often applied at non-insulated buildings, such as car parks.

A third and final variant (type C) took inspiration from old city walls and quay walls on which vegetation grows directly in the joints or on the bricks. Modern, insulated facades require a new type of outer cavity leaf in which, for example, interconnected holes with substrate are applied.

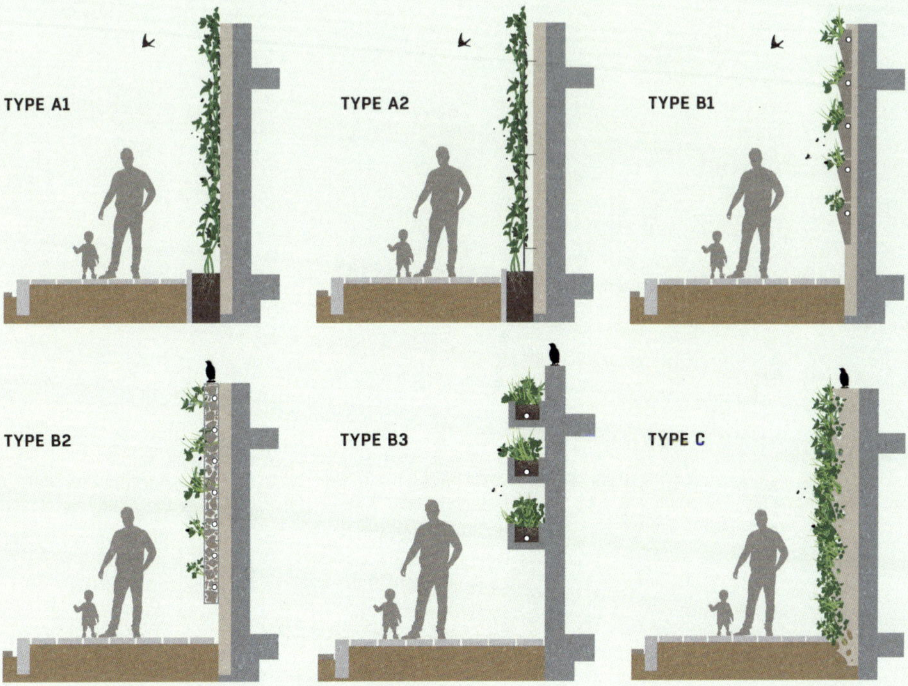

Typology Transitional Space

Accommodation spaces that are transitions between the inner and outer environment provide opportunities as spaces for humans and nature to share. Balconies and terraces can have small-scale architectural elements such as pergolas and cable constructions for plants to attach themselves to. On a larger scale, special indoor/outdoor spaces such as atria, overarching pergolas or net-shaped envelopments can form transitional spaces between the conditioned indoor climate and 'outside'. Spaces for plants, but also for insects and birds.

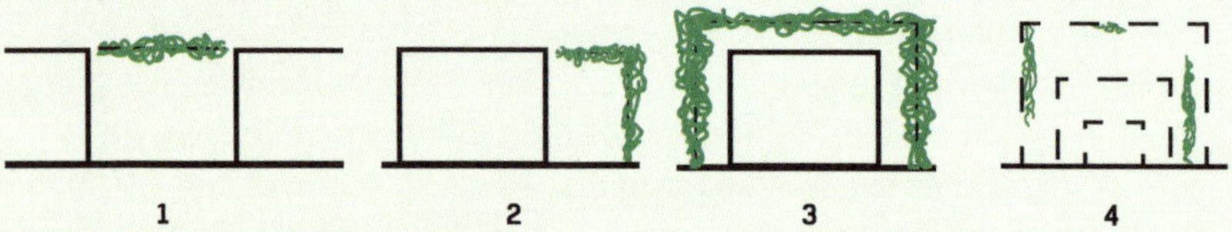

Transitional Zone

Allowing nature into our immediate living environment is a big step, especially when it comes to independently functioning ecosystems. We humans are accustomed to a precisely conditioned indoor climate, with the exactly right temperature, air quality and humidity. By dividing the transitional space into zones, a transition between the outdoor and indoor climate can be created instead of having a strict separation between the two, like layers around a closed core that each have specific physical and visual functions.

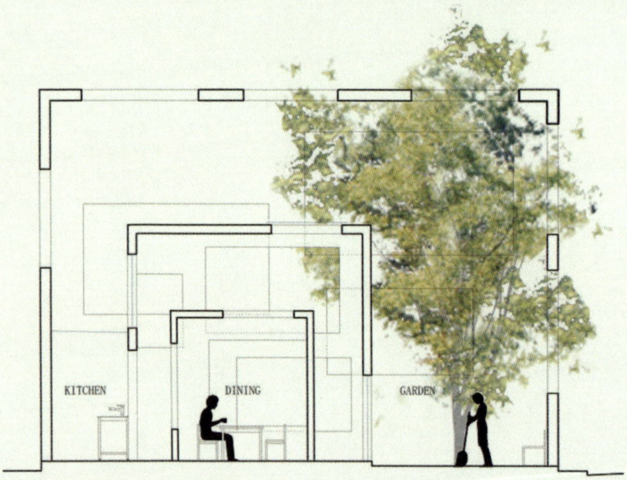

Above: House N, Tokyo, Sou Fujimoto, 2008, JP / Top right: 1. ATRIUM: Lumen, Wageningen, Behnisch Architekten, 1998, NL / ATRIUM: MFO-Park, Zürich, Burckhard Architektur, 2002, CH / 2. PERGOLA: Bus station, Heerlen, Michel Huisman, 2008, NL / 3. NET-SHAPED ENVELOPMENT: student accommodation, München, Fink+Jocher, 2005, D / 4. ZONES: House N, Tokyo, Sou Fujimoto, 2008, JP

From top left to bottom right: Virginia creeper (self-attacher) / Honey suckle (creeper) / Old man's beard (ranker) / Winter jasmin (support climber) / Below left: wisteria up to 15 meters high / Below right: ivy.

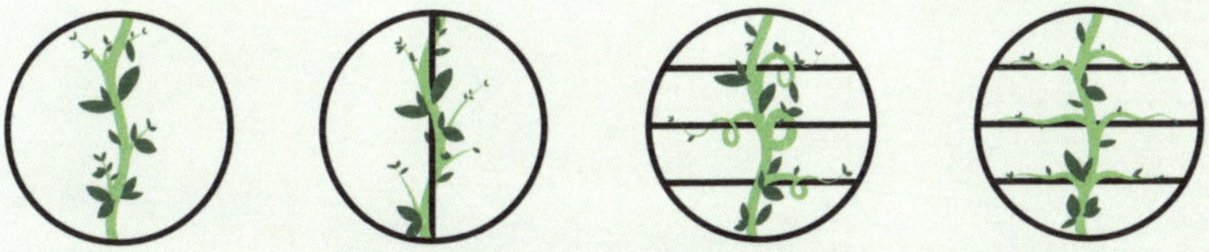

SELF-ATTACHERS CREEPERS RANKER SUPPORT CLIMBER

Choosing climbing plants

When choosing climbing plants, there are three important aspects to consider:
- height: some species of climbing plants grow taller than others.
- the flowering period: different species flower at different times of the year.
- the orientation: depending on full sun, semi-shade or shade, certain types of climbing plants are more suitable than others.

The starting point is to always choose native species and a substrate that matches the soil type found in the area.

For plants climbing up from the open ground along the facade, a distinction can be made between self-attachers, creepers and vines/support-climbers. Self-attachers, such as ivy and Virginia creeper, adhere directly to the outer leaf. Creepers such as honeysuckle and wisteria wind themselves around previously installed vertical cables. Vines and support-climbers seek foothold on both horizontal and vertical battens or grids, with vines such as traveller's joy and passionflower using their tendrils. Support-climbers such as firethorn and jasmine lean on horizontal elements such as cables. Due to the absence of tendrils, it is necessary to attach support climbers to the underlying structure.

Self-attachers have a bad name because the roots are said to damage masonry and woodwork. Ivy and creeper in particular, seek out cracks and holes to attach themselves to the structure behind. Where lime-rich mortar has been applied, the pointing can be damaged, which can be prevented with modern concrete mortar. Roots can also creep behind the woodwork, causing damage.

Proper detailing combined with maintenance of climbing plants can prevent this. (see image bottom right: Het Funen, Geurst & Schulze. 2007, NL)

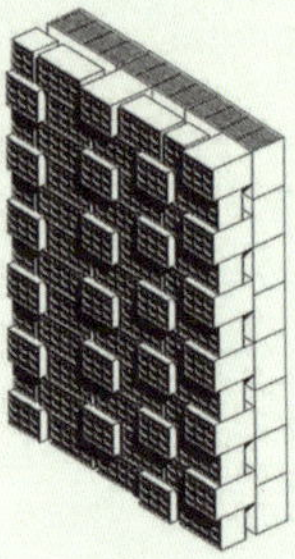

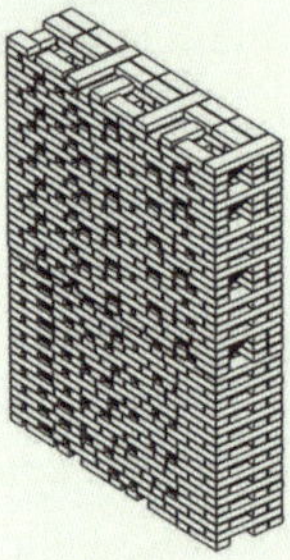

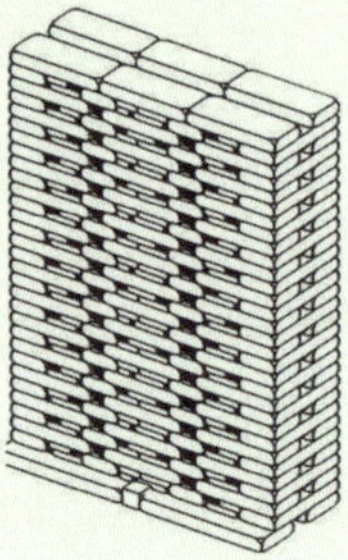

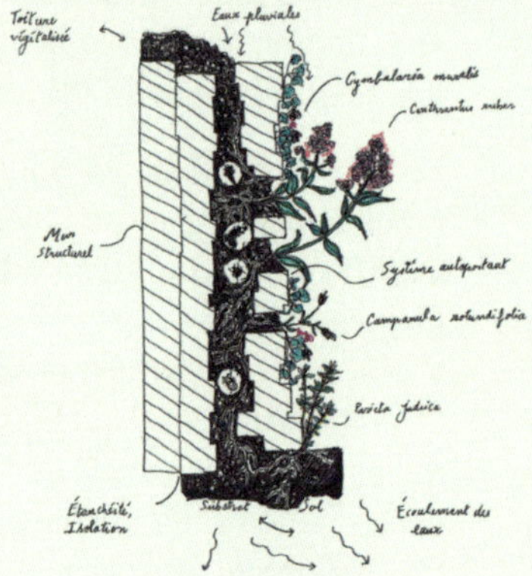

Biodiversity Wall

Rue Buffon, Paris, ChartierDalix, 2021, FR

The 'biodiversity wall' is an experimental vertical green wall designed to promote biodiversity in inner cities. Instead of the vertical, hydroponic 'living walls' usually planted with exotic plants, this wall is developed to house local and native fauna and flora that can establish themselves autonomously. A family of prototypes using three different materials has been placed in Rue Buffon in Paris. Inspired by traditional stone walls on which vegetation grows spontaneously, the third prototype was built with reused and recycled stones from various locations in Paris. A distinctive feature is that substrate has been placed in the openings of the masonry joints, which, through direct contact with the soil around the wall, provides a natural substrate for the planting. The project is part of a research project and will be monitored throughout the different seasons.

Bioreceptive Concrete

Respyre, NL

Inspired by the greenery on old quay walls and ruins, designers and materials scientists are working on new building products. One example is bioreceptive concrete, a porous material that can retain moisture for mosses to grow, which can then serve as a habitat for micro-organisms. The material is still in the experimental phase with promising test plots. The slow growth of plants requires time, also because mosses are difficult to sow and lichens and hard to cultivate. Only a few species of mosses suitable for concrete grow in the city such as redshank moss, wall screw-moss, grey-cushioned grimmia and silver moss. Bioreceptive concrete is currently still being tested but appears to offer various benefits, such as absorbing CO_2, improving the microclimate and increasing the insulation value of the facade. One of the first products consisted of three layers: the outer layer traps water, the middle layer retains water, and the inner layer is waterproof to protect the structure behind. The load-bearing properties of the material are limited, but it can be reinforced with, for instance, basalt. The environmental footprint is low because 50-100 per cent recycled concrete is used as substrate material. Also, a low fraction of cement enhances the bioreceptive qualities.

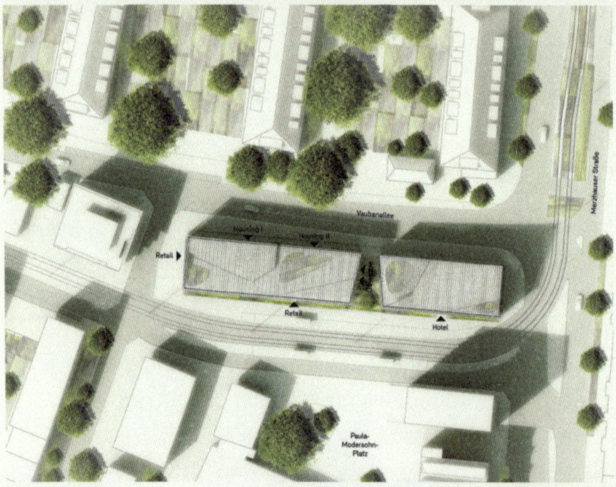
Merzhauser Straße
Vaubanallee
Housing I
Housing II
Retail
Retail
Hotel
Paula-
Modersohn-
Platz

Stadthaus M1

Freiburg, Barkow+Leibinger, 2013, D

Planting can be used to create a zone between the outdoor climate and the conditioned indoor climate. Stadthaus M1 is a good example of this. The complex consists of two volumes with a pocket park between the two buildings. The higher part on the east side contains a hotel, while the other contains flats with shops on the ground floor. A screen shelters the loggias and balconies on the south facade, as well as the facades facing the pocket park. Plants grow from the full soil along stainless steel vertical cables attached separately from the facades. The screen, covered with climbing plants such as wisteria, clematis, honeysuckle and climbing roses provides food, shelter and nesting opportunities for birds, bats and insects. It also acts as additional shading as the leaves cast shade on the building in the summer months, while the deciduous plants let sunlight through in the cold winter months.

Left: Facade with various types of climbing plants / Situation / Ensemble of residential building and hotel with passage / Transitional zone / Below: Cross-section of the facade with cables for facade greening / Horizontal facade detail with cables at a distance of 50 cm of the facade.

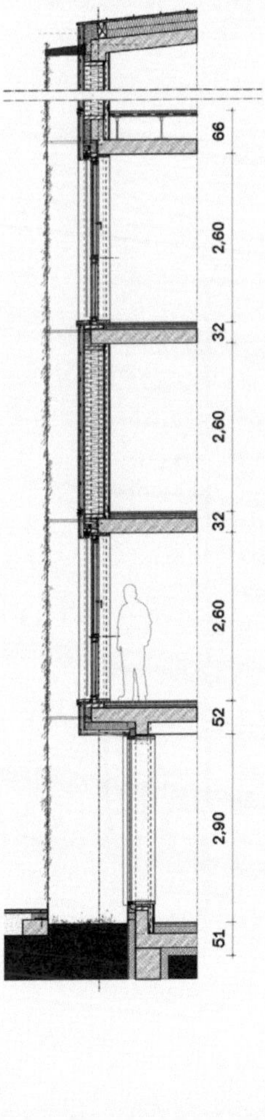

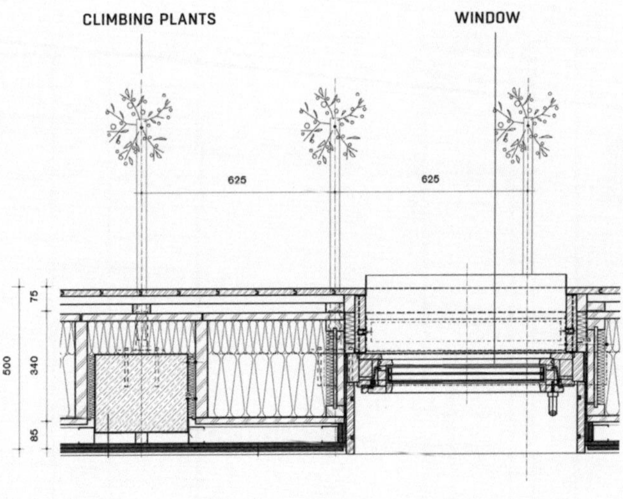

M6B2 Tower of Biodiversity

Paris, Maison Édouard François, 2016, FR

Together with a lower building volume, this 50-metre-high residential building is part of an urban ensemble in Paris. The design premise was to actively use the tower to enhance local biodiversity. Key features include planting on the roof, a garden at the base of the building that flows into the facade, equipped with nets for plants to grow up along, and trees in specially designed tubes in the facade.

Along these nets on the facade, (climbing) plants and trees grow at different rates. First, the fast climbers will overgrow the facade, followed by the slower-growing shrubs. Finally, the slow-growing trees will determine the appearance. Not only will the building continuously change in appearance due to the planting, the moiré effect of the titanium cladding also produces a subtle layering.
The most innovative part are the tubes that have been specially designed for the building in which trees can grow. Together with a botanist, a selection was made of trees with habitats in a rocky environment. Research has shown that the growth rate and health levels of the trees are therefore higher than in a conventional tree container. Seeds for the plants on the roof were collected from the Paris area. Aided by the wind and altitude, the seeds can subsequently spread around the city.

Right: Continuous zone of balconies/ Garden at the foot of the tower / Trees, including summer oaks, five years after planting / Ensemble with inner courtyard / Garden at the base of the building.
Below: Cross-sections.

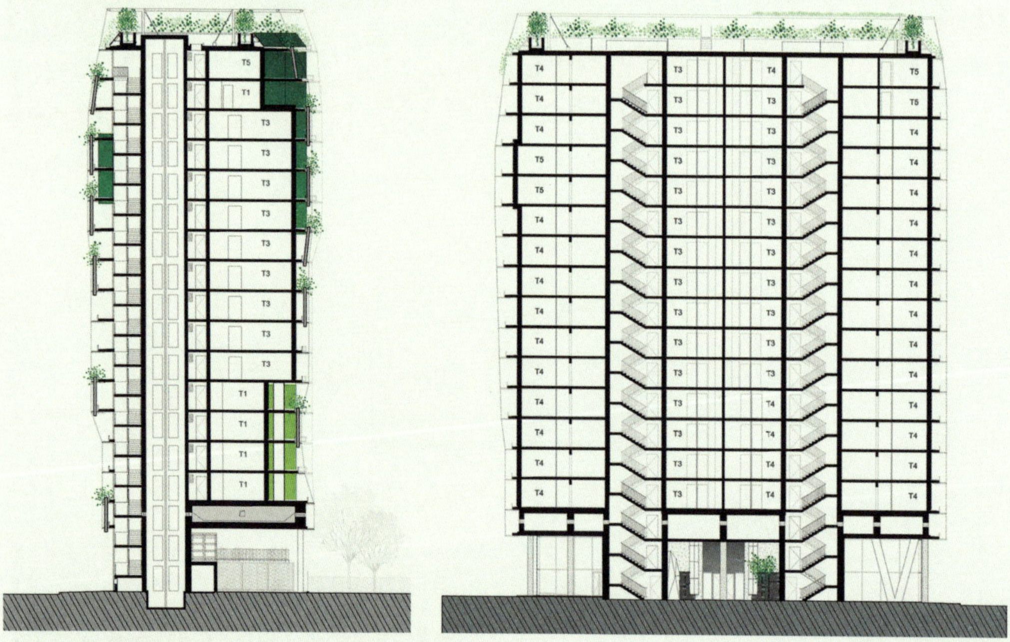

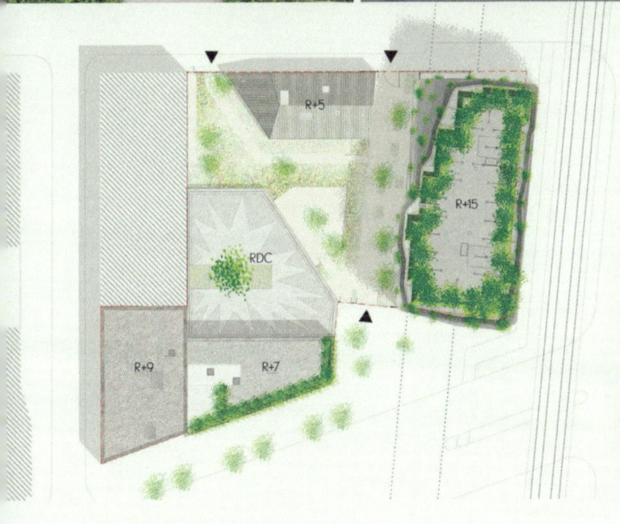
R+5
R+15
RDC
R+9
R+7

Above: Net stocking facade enveloping the M6B2 Tower of Biodiversity / Roofgarden / Below: The seedbomb effect projected on the map of Paris.

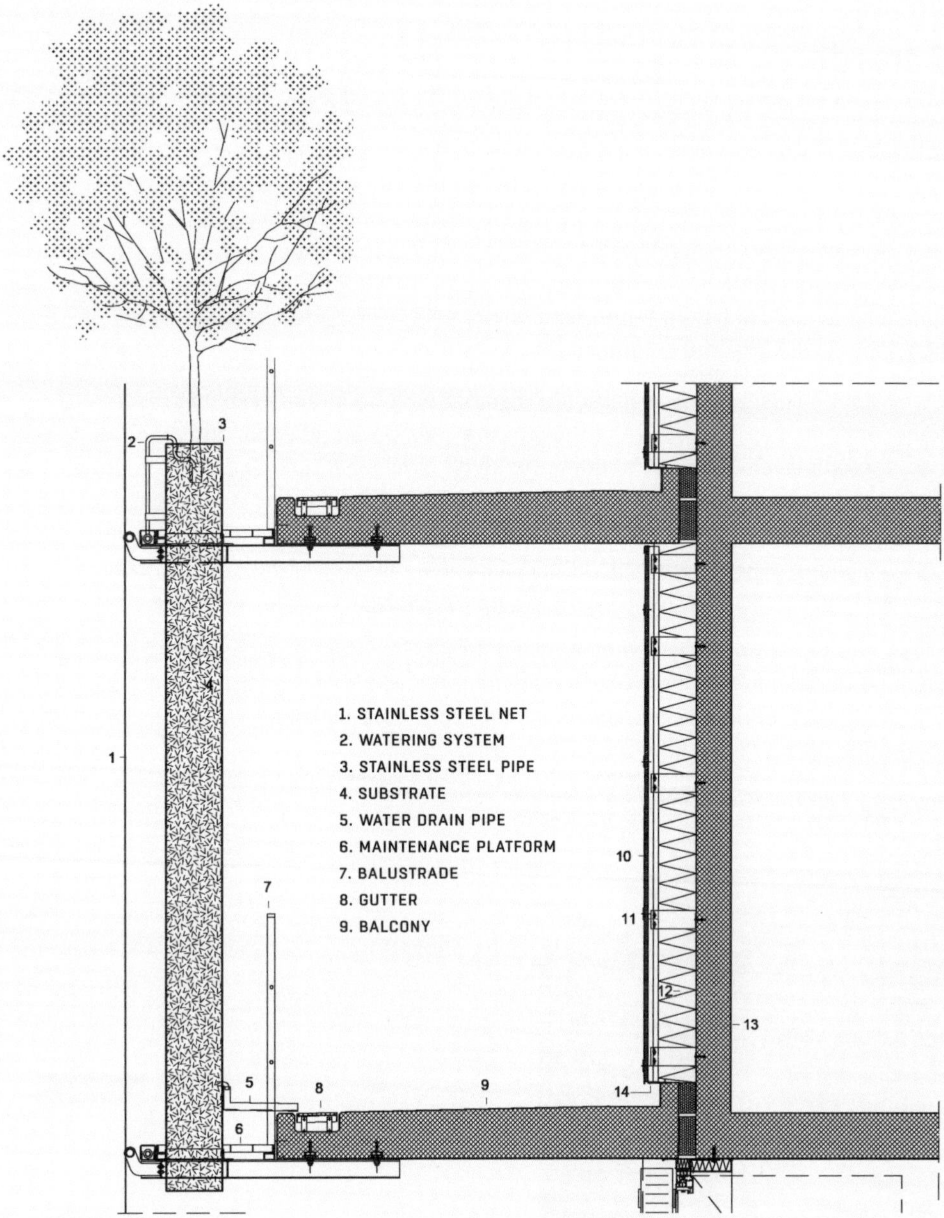

Above: Cross section balcony / Left below: M6B2 Tower of Biodiversity as seed bomb: the wind enables the seed of plants on the roof to spread across the city.

25 Verde

Turin, Luciano Pia, 2012, IT

Residential building 25 Verde is a green oasis in Turin's stony city centre. Architect Luciano Pia designed a green transition between the city and the 63 apartments. This zone includes ponds on the ground floor, green outdoor spaces and terraces topped with trees and plants in large containers. Deciduous vegetation has been used, allowing sufficient sunlight into the houses in winter while providing shade in summer. The planting is now as tall as 8 metres in some places and offers a wide variety of foliage shapes, colours and inflorescences.

The U-shaped building forms a courtyard together with an already existing residential building. Both the courtyard and the roofs of the building are planted. The green roof has a substrate layer 60 to 100 centimetres thick to allow shrubs and trees to grow. As owners, the residents of the upper floors are responsible for the maintenance of the roof. They have set up part of the roof as an orchard. The roof package provides thermal insulation and absorbs and filters rainwater, minimizing the need for artificial irrigation. It also slows rainwater runoff to ground level.

The load-bearing structure is designed like a forest. The steel trees support the wooden terraces and, together with the planting, the whole structure forms not only a habitat for insects and birds but, above all, an expressive building.

Right: Green conclave in stony part of Turin / Terrace at one of the apartments / Below: Corten steel planting containers with a diameter of 2 to 4 metres for trees that can grow up to 8 metres high / Cross-section over transitional zone.

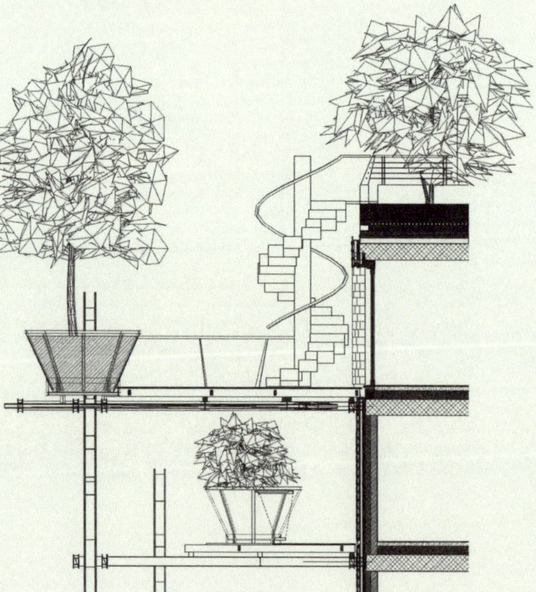

SUND Nature Park

Copenhagen, SLA Landscape architects, 2018, DK

Maersk Tower is a new research complex located in the middle of SUND Nature Park, a completely new city park in Copenhagen's Nørrebro district. The park is part of the campus of Copenhagen University and at the same time offers a wide range of natural, functional and social functions to the surrounding city.

A 5000 m² roof landscape has been designed to allow nature to develop by itself. The roof has been designed with a great diversity of native plants and trees. Sixty species of grasses and herbs, typical of the surrounding meadows, have been planted on the low green roofs immediately surrounding the tower. The building has its own water processing installation which makes abundant rainwater and greywater fit for flushing toilets and irrigating the gardens. It is designed to be able to cope with extreme rainfall events that potentially occur only once every hundred years.

With hawthorns and oak trees, SUND Nature Park refers to Copenhagen's old, public Græsningsfælled (Grassland), which until the 1840s ran all the way from the countryside to Sankt Hans Torv. Also, the park features a large number of exotic tree species with different cultural and biological origins, as a tribute to multicultural Nørrebro. The mix of foreign and native trees and plants not only makes the park's urban nature richer and more varied to look at, smell and experience, but it also makes the park more resilient and thus more robust in the face of future climate change.

The lower roofs are accessible from both the building and the park, allowing the city's flora and fauna to be experienced up close. A distinctive feature is the bicycle bridge that offers a view of the green roofs and a landscape rich in biodiversity.

Left: Green roof landscape / Pedestrian bridge over roof landscape/ Sunken entrance to bicycle parking under the main building / Below: Situation.

Amstelstroom Bridge

Amsterdam, VenhoevenCS architecture+urbanism, Smartland, 2022, NL

Amsterdam's canals are world-famous. Less well known is the significance of the network for nature in the city. With several projects, the City of Amsterdam is working to improve the water system. In the tender for a new bridge near the Amstel, it was explicitly stated that the design should also be of significance for urban wildlife. The winning team of architect, landscape architect and ecological consultant created a crossing and habitat for humans, plants and animals. For insects, the bridge is a stepping stone, a connection from the Amstelscheg to the new neighbourhood on the other side that includes Park Somerlust. In the central axis between the lanes, a broad strip with herbs has been created that attract bees, butterflies and bumblebees.

Behind the side of the bridge, there are entrance openings with nest boxes for various types of birds, including tits, sparrows, swifts, starlings and jackdaws. Small birds generally do not like to brood in nests behind large openings: the smallest are for tits and the largest for jackdaws. Nesting sites for kingfishers and sand martins have been created in the pylons of the bridge close to the water.

Elongated holes have been made in the piers, to be used by bats as a nursery. Crevices have been left open between the concrete slabs of the bridge. Slightly roughened, these are suitable as summer quarters for bats. In addition, bowl-shaped nesting sites for barn swallows and house martins have been installed under the bridge.

Holes have been drilled at the top of the bridge's red brick pylons. In the relatively warm bricks, wild bees and other insects can lay their eggs.

Measures have also been taken for aquatic life. A bed of crushed rock has been laid on top of the concrete foundation. A jumbled bottom to which marine life can attach and where the bullhead feels at home. In addition, cage structures with wood have been installed. These allow freshwater polyps, sponges, aquatic insects, caddisflies and other water insect to settle. It also makes a suitable substrate for water-purifying zebra mussels. These, in turn, are food for fish such as perch, carp and pike-perch.

Right: Connection from the Amstelscheg to the new neighbourhood with a native flower-rich road median / Details of the bridge with integrated nesting facilities / Left bottom: Nest holes for insects were drilled in the red brick masonry of the pylons of the bridge / Below: Situation.

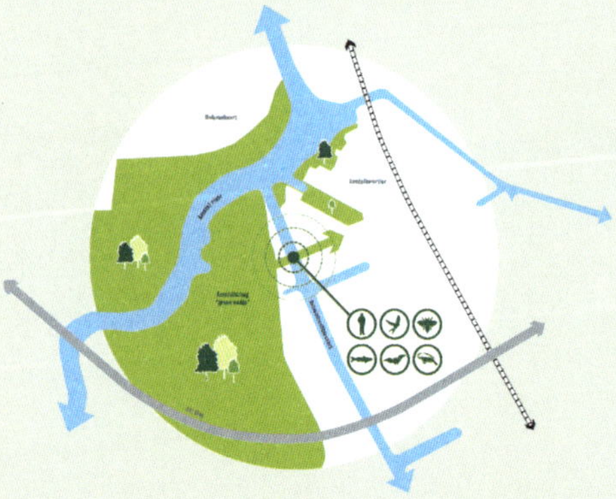

New Quay Systems

The Dutch water city is characterized by canals with stony quays, on which a unique biotope has developed over the ages. When quays are renovated, this biotope is in danger of disappearing and to prevent this, several experimental quay walls have been developed. In Amsterdam, a nature-inclusive quay wall has been developed. The focus is on creating conditions for nature to establish itself independently. The quay wall will be widely implemented in Amsterdam in the coming years, occasionally adding planting for immediate result and appearance.

Breda experimented with a quay construction from which trees could grow. Other experiments involve a wide joint, grouted with lime-enriched mortar. Tests are done with substrate in a 40mm cavity. Additionally, there are quay elements where gaps between the stones allow water to pass through in the cavity.

In Delft, the choice was made not to bring back the existing flora, but to create a new biotope. Behind the open masonry of so-called clickbrick, a 50 mm thick substrate was installed. A cover plate allows water to moisten the substrate. This creates a vertical green wall at the water's edge on which plants can attach.

The 'Utrechtse Steen' has prefabricated holes in the front of the brick and is made of a type of clay with moisture-accumulating properties. The holes are not through-and-through but only eight centimetres deep. This allows moisture from behind the quay wall to reach the roots of the plants through about 20 millimetres of brick. The holes with different diameters are provided with plugs of lime-rich substrate so that plants found in the quay walls further along find a similar substrate in the new quays.

Left: Green quay walls, Amsterdam, Municipality of Amsterdam, 2020, NL / Utrechtse Steen, Amersfoort, Ruimtelab, 2021, NL / Wall Garden, Delft / Green Quays, Breda / Traditional quay wall / Below: Cross-section Green quay walls, Amsterdam.

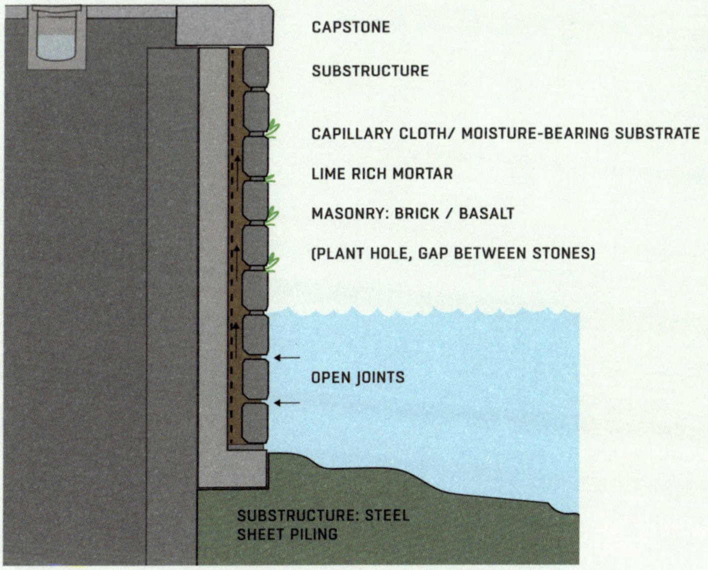

Building Hazards

Glass

For almost all birds, glass facades and other highly reflective surfaces can be a hazard. Many birds become window victims because they do not recognize the reflective surface as an object in time, but see it as a free flight path. This happens especially when the glass surface reflects the sky and greenery from the immediate surroundings, causing the bird to think it can fly on. Research shows that about half of bird crashes against glass result in the death of the animal.

There are several solutions to this problem. Glass with visible patterns on bird-friendly glass with ingrained UV patterns that most birds can, but humans cannot, see. Most effective is a dense line pattern, lines 2 centimetres thick but no longer than 30 centimetres on every 10 centimetres. Milk glass can also help in situations where many birds fly and the application of patterns with solar cells incorporated in the glass can also be effective. If a reflective facade is nevertheless desired, tall vegetation, trees and shrubs should be avoided in front of the glass, otherwise birds will think they are flying into a green area and may fly into the reflective surface. This applies especially to the bottom 15 metres of a building.

Artificial light

For many animals, artificial light is a negative factor. Birds, bats and insects such as moths can get confused by artificial light. It causes flight paths to be interrupted, disrupts hormones and thus the day-night cycle, insects may keep flying near a lamp instead of foraging and lighting makes species extra vulnerable as prey causing them to lose habitat, for example. While there are animals that can benefit from artificial light, for most species the effect is negative and thus it is disruptive to the overall ecosystem. This problem is often easy to avoid with good design and adaptation of human behaviour. In terms of behaviour, one choice is to turn off lights in office buildings, business premises and shops at night. Illumination of walls, logos and other advertising at night can also be limited, in favour of biodiversity. In terms of design, luminaires can be used that only illuminate the road, preventing stray light to adjacent greenery. Where possible, lights can be installed at low positions, for example in a bridge railing where the light shines only on the road surface and not on the water. Light intensity can also determine the degree of disturbance to animals or the range of light pollution:

Artificial lights in the city are in excess.

Brown long-eared bat with insulation material in its fur: this animal could just about escape from the cavity wall but it did not survive the later insulation. Many bats will never be able to leave the cavity wall and lose places to stay, which will have negative consequences for the population.

dimmed light is therefore recommended when lighting cannot be avoided. The effect of the colour of light (its wavelength) on animals is currently still the subject of much research: warmer light seems to be less disruptive for both animals and humans. Blue and UV-rich light is generally the most disruptive for all species.

Post-insulation

All species that use the outer shell of the building, so those that reside in the cavity wall or under the tiled roof, are threatened by post-insulation. Post-insulation is done in existing buildings when the energy performance of the building is low and needs to be improved. In this way, tens of thousands of homes are insulated every year, eliminating habitats for animals, or in the worst case, they are injured or killed in the process. This has a negative impact on the population and creates scarcity of habitat for the species that depend on the building and face loss of nesting opportunities. This particularly affects bats and birds, which use the cavity or space under roof tiles to roost. To reduce this negative effect, alternative places to live are needed in a higher supply than will be removed. This takes time, as animals have a habituation period to discover and start using a new roost: preferably several years and preferably as close to the original roost as possible because animals have site fidelity. Work should subsequently be carried out when animals are no longer present, in other words outside the breeding season or the period when bats use a building. To this end, there are methods for making a building 'nature-free' in advance to avoid injuring and killing species. But this cannot be done overnight. Destroying, damaging or disturbing habitats can require an exemption or dispensation from the prohibitions of nature conservation laws. This can be granted subject to conditions, if the negative impact can be demonstrably limited and the situation does not ultimately deteriorate or even improve. This is precisely

An ecologist carries out an inventory: monitoring is of great importance in monitoring the effectiveness of measures.

why nature-inclusive construction is very important, so that there are sufficient roosts available for building-related species.

Species Management Plan

In this context, many city-wide studies on building-bound species in relation to energy performance improvements (such as post-insulation) and spatial developments are currently underway in the Netherlands. This concept is called Species Management Plan. Its purpose is to map protected situations on a large scale (network of bat roosts and nests of a number of bird species) and thus create a long-term plan with ground rules for renovation and new construction to ensure that the populations of protected species do not decline. Nature-inclusive renovation and construction is an obligation here, whereby monitoring will determine whether measures are truly effective or require adjustment.

Detailing bird stop

Animal-proofing devices, such as eaves closures (sometimes called bird stops) against nesting under a tiled roof, are obviously better omitted. If they are needed anyway, at least provide a smaller area where birds can nest. For example, place the eaves closures a few rows of tiles higher up in the roof.

6

If you have built castles in the air, your work need not be lost; that is where they should be. Now put the foundations under them.

HENRY DAVID THOREAU

Ten Recommendations for Nature-inclusive Design

There is still a world to explore and win for the nature-inclusive designer. Building Urban Nature at this stage of development of the nature-inclusive design practice cannot really be much more than a book of inspiration and an exploration of ecological principles. Nevertheless, it is possible to formulate some general pointers that focus mainly on a design attitude and can help in navigating this journey of discovery. We therefore conclude the book with some recommendations or design rules.

1. DESIGN A PROCESS, enable urban nature

Nature-inclusive design is primarily about initiating and sustaining nature development in buildings and cities. It is about creating the right conditions for an ecological process and realizing a green pattern or image. Nature cannot be drawn up in advance. For much natural greenery, creating the right habitat conditions for the desired group of cohesive species is therefore more important than planting a specific species in a 'designed' spot. The natural process takes over after the building is completed, based on the biotic and abiotic conditions—whether designed or not—that are present. From an ecological perspective, it is about inviting nature and then letting things go.

Because of this need to think (also and especially) in processes, nature-inclusive design differs from more traditional architecture and urban planning. Indeed, these are maintained precisely so as not to evolve over time to a non-predicted state.

In that respect, it is not so much about *making* urban nature, but about *enabling* it, about setting natural processes in motion. Not to simply let nature take its course, because the context is urban and human-made. It therefore requires a form of mediation between the human-made and the natural; a nature-culture fusion.

2. ACT STRATEGICALLY, look for biobased solutions

The process-oriented aspect of nature-inclusive design also means that you have to act strategically. The trade-off of interests is one such strategy. To take an example from water management: breaching a river dyke is not in itself specifically (nature)-friendly, but in the long run it produces richer nature through the creation of wetlands, while

Cutaway of a nautilus shell showing the chambers.

simultaneously dealing with excessively high water levels due to climate change 'for free' (or vice versa, depending on the priorities of the various partners). In this way, an alliance is forged between two usually opposed parties, the engineers and the nature lovers, whose opposing interests often frustrate the development process. For the nature-inclusive designer. The secondary goals that are added 'for free' by creating more green space and other ecological measures—the ecosystem services often mentioned in this book—as well as the economic benefits, are also an important strategic tool in negotiating with other building partners and policymakers about the space and budget needed for nature development.

Be tactical and never explain ecological features as a (necessary) addition to the design, but rather as obvious and indispensable parts of the whole. A priority can be set for each urban area or building section, nature here, culture there. In this way, not every public space or building section becomes a compromise of all functions. There are always cultural, ecological, recreational and liveability aspects to each place and it is wise to make a strategic choice, reasoned from the bigger picture, of what to prioritize in which place. This will encourage a diversity of developments and give greater value to the whole.

3. DESIGN INCLUSIVELY AND INTEGRALLY, forwards and backwards

A design brief purely for nature development will rarely be given. It is therefore important to 'include' nature, or rather conditions for nature, in other projects. The city is always redeveloping somewhere and that is where opportunities for urban nature arise. Those opportunities can be cashed in the moment decisions are made and built; integrally and from the very beginning of the decision-making and design process. From the smallest renovation job to major urban plans, a nature function can always be integrated into it. The smart nature-inclusive designer is alert to these opportunities and has an arsenal of possible nature inclusions on hand to bring them to the table when the time is right.

Even if the brief does involve the exclusive design of building-based or urban nature, it makes sense, where relevant and meaningful, to take the opposite route and seek integration with the stony city and human functions. Also think in reverse; what does nature gain from this purely human function? Integration will only make both spheres stronger.

In industrial processes, we have forward and backward integration. Forward integration is the inclusion of process parts that follow *after* the main process, backward integration refers to the inclusion of process parts that take place *before* the main process. It is no different in the nature-inclusive design and building process: forward nature integration concerns the inclusion in the design of subsequent growth processes and maintenance; backward nature integration is the inclusion of existing, local natural processes and of the moment of decision in the design and implementation phase.

4. KEEP IT SIMPLE, but create complexity

The resilience of an ecological system is largely determined by complexity and diversity. Therefore, look for opportunities for gradients and integrate habitats for different species. Nature benefits from a great diversity of (urban) elements and thrives better in a complex system. Simplicity, singularity, homogeneity and order may work for some architectural styles, but for the nature-inclusive style, if there is such a thing, it does not

work. This is not to say designing a complex and diverse system means that the design itself has to be extremely complicated and multiform. On the contrary; keep the design simple if necessary, but ensure complexity and diversity in use.
Remember, too, that barren, dry, food- and species-poor areas are also important. Diversity in the supply of such biotopes is important, both as pioneering sites and as sanctuaries for species that actually need these 'poor' conditions. Green roofs can also play an important role in this, for instance as 'brown' stepping stones.

5. DESIGN A COHERENT SYSTEM, think in planes, lines and points
Installing a nest box for a bird species makes little sense if the additional necessary provisions, such as shelter, sufficient food, connections and variety, are not also considered. It is always about fitting into the overall system or creating a more or less complete subsystem in connection with that system. The micro-scale of a small habitat (the points) should be connected by various routes (the lines) to the macro-scale of the larger biotopes and/or green areas, including natural areas in and around the city (the planes).
Large and small and the connection between them are important, even for non-natural designs. What good is a building without a street to reach it, and what good is a street if it leads nowhere? What good is a maternity roost for bats if the passage leading to it is nailed shut? What good is a roost if there is no water and greenery nearby to drink and eat? There is strength in cohesion!

6. DESIGN WITH NATURE, design 'lazy' and contextually
Don't make it harder for yourself than you have to and design with nature. Most of it is already there and the process aspect means that you rarely start from scratch. So make the building especially inviting to species of plants and animals already present in the environment. A certain 'laziness' in adding new nature provisions or new species too enthusiastically can be productive. And do not clear out everything in order to start with a clean slate: spare the existing soil and greenery and leave them intact as much as possible during the construction process. Find out what the building can add at that location and design solutions that connect the present with the future. Make contextual and site-specific designs. In doing so, see the various natural elements as fully-fledged 'building materials' with their own architectural significance.

7. DRAW INSPIRATION FROM NATURE AND CULTURE, but stay true to your own discipline
Look outside the field of ecology and biology for inspiring solutions and concepts as well. Many artists and industrial designers 'work' with nature. From an ecological point of view, there may be some things to criticize about such work, but be open to it, it may provide an unexpected direction or an as-yet unimagined solution for designs that do work ecologically.
Also look at ecological systems and biological principles outside the city and examine whether they 'fit' into the urban whole. Pay attention to recent design fashions such as biomimicry or biomimetic design. While these movements mainly produce pretty images, and by no means always ecologically sound buildings, look at them anyway, pick up the good ideas and concepts, and make sure that in your own nature-inclusive design, they are indeed ecologically sound and will really work.

But also realize that design (the city and the building) and its associated ecology are not the same as 'real' nature or the arts; inspiration is not the same as imitation. Inspiration acts from its own discipline, imitation denies the uniqueness of building and design.

8. DESIGN THE MANAGEMENT and manage the design

Include future management in the design and involve the manager in planning at an early stage. Determine together what is practically possible or necessary. For example, water collection on the roof can help irrigate plants in the building. Also check whether the design can be managed within the available budget in such a way that the final goal can be achieved. Especially with greenery on buildings, height and drought determine whether planting will survive or not. Management can also indicate what is not desirable in the light of nuisance or unmanageable elements. So, accompany the design with a management plan, especially if it is a project where local residents play a role in the management.

But also think in reverse (integrate backwards). All too often, special abseiling gardeners have to be called in to trim the protruding branches of a tree on the balcony. A backwards-designing ecotect realizes this and designs in such a way that those branches don't get there in the first place anyway.

9. TAKE A POSITION IN NATURE DEVELOPMENT DISCUSSIONS and thus create support

The right attitude to nature development and management is also an issue among ecologists. Should an ecosystem be protected from invasion by exotic species? Or should these exotics instead be assumed to be part of the natural development process? On a building, do you want to keep out feral pigeons, jackdaws and gulls or is it okay for them to be there too? Do residents actually like a natural and wild roof garden on their building? This debate is held at the city level but applies equally to a small stepping stone like a green roof. It is always wise to define one's own position as a designer in such social, societal and/or cultural discussions. Without taking one's own stance, the design will be less outspoken, and therefore may garner less support. And if there is no support, nature-inclusive measures are the first to be dropped in a round of cuts. Always be sure to communicate well in this regard: Why was a particular measure or attitude chosen?

10. HANG IN THERE and keep going

None of it is easy, when it comes to nature-inclusive design, but it is incredibly inspiring, satisfying, and ultimately an absolute necessity.

Torre Guinigi, Lucca, IT

ECOLOGICAL TERMS
(explained for architects)

ecology The science that studies the relationships between living organisms, such as plants and animals, and their inanimate (abiotic) environment. It looks at the interaction between organisms (how do species interact with each other or what influence does one species have on another) and the interaction with their habitat. In ecology, associated processes and patterns are additionally studied at different scales.

---

urban ecology A separate discipline that studies nature within the urban context. This includes human activities and the built environment as major factors of influence. There is no specific demarcation of the discipline, but it is characterized by a high degree of paving, buildings and human activity. Within urban ecology, much attention is paid to urban planning, management and human interactions.

Earth System Science A very young, interdisciplinary science that studies the cycles of the planet (from atmosphere to lithosphere, from biosphere to noösphere, and between disciplines such as biology, geochemistry, economics, meteorology et cetera among themselves) including their effects on the planet as a whole. This includes climate change and all other impacts of human activity on the Earth.

---

critical zone The zone in which life on Earth takes place. Which, on the scale of the planet, is only a thin layer of a few tens of metres (on which humans and plants depend directly). When earth layers with deep water down to the air we breathe are included, that zone is about 230 metres thick. It is the layer in which all kinds of processes and interactions take place, distinguishing atmosphere, hydrosphere, biosphere and geosphere, which make life possible and form our world as we know it today.

---

ecosystem A complex, self-regulating community of living organisms and the physical factors of their environment. It includes both biotic and abiotic elements within a specific area and the interactions between these components. A pond is an example of a relatively small ecosystem, an ocean an example of a large one.

ecotope A spatial, physical environment in which an animal or plant community lives and interacts. Multiple species' habitats may be present in an ecotope. An ecotope focuses on the way organisms live and interact within a part of the ecosystem. An example of an ecotope is a forest: within it, different habitats can be found (such as a squirrel's habitat and a woodpecker's habitat).

---

biotope An environment containing a biological community. It is the complete habitat of that or those species, including climatic conditions and soil. Biotope is a broader concept than ecotope: a biotope may contain several ecotopes. When a biotope is defined, all abiotic factors are also described in relation to the community of organisms.

---

community A group of different species of plants or animals, or both, that interact with each other within a given geographical area. These can be very complex relationships, such as an entire food chain or a forest community of many species of animals and plants together.

---

habitat The physical habitat of a species. In this place, the species finds everything it needs to survive, the five conditions for settlement described in the book. A species' habitat describes where it lives and what role it plays in that area.

---

niche A role or place assumed by an animal or plant species in an ecosystem. This includes everything to do with its way of life: from interaction with other species to food choice, and from all physical conditions placed on its environment to its behaviour. Each species functions optimally in its own niche. When species have similar niches, competition arises, which in turn can sometimes lead to adaptations of a species.

---

refugium An isolated area that acts as protection for a population. It is a refuge, temporary or otherwise, in an environment that is unfavourable at the time. A refugium can thus ensure the survival of a species and, for example, be used as a resource once the environment has improved again for the species. A city can be a refugium for some species when it is located in an area poor in biodiversity.

succession An ecological process involving a noticeable change in species composition within an ecosystem. Biological communities succeed each other in sequence. Within a certain time frame, a stable biological community may develop (for instance, the development from pioneer vegetation to a climax forest).

habitat gradation The process by which a habitat changes to a different type. This can be triggered by natural processes, but also by human activity. An example is succession, where in an area animals and plants succeed each other (such as from young and species-poor, to old and species-rich forest). It also includes natural processes such as erosion and sedimentation. Anthropogenic examples are climate change, fragmentation by agriculture or urbanization. Habitat degradation is the negative variant of habitat gradation.

gradient A gradual transition between different biotopes. For example, a gradual transition in biotic and abiotic environmental conditions, or a gradual transition in the mix of species where communities overlap. Nature-inclusive design is mainly concerned with the first example: (creating) gradual transitions of biotic conditions on a relatively small, local scale. For instance, a hill (from shadow to sunlight, from low to high), a bush between a field with herbs and a tree, a transition from humid to dry, and so on. Gradients enhance local biodiversity.

biota All organisms in an ecosystem, including animals, plants, fungi and micro-organisms in a given region. It is sometimes used in the description of an ecosystem to indicate its living part.

biotic - abiotic factors All environmental factors that involve life are biotic. All non-living environmental factors are called abiotic (such as climate, soil conditions, water composition).

population A group of individuals of one species, living together within certain boundaries (such as of a forest, or a city). A population is capable of reproducing itself.

ecological stepping stone A small, isolated habitat that can function as a link between two larger areas. This allows species to move more easily between the two larger areas.

foraging Finding, gathering and eating food.

biodiversity Literally: biological diversity. This roughly includes three components: the diversity of all living organisms (such as unicellular organisms, fungi, plants, animals), diversity in genes (variation in genetic information) and diversity in ecosystems.

symbiosis A close interaction between two different types of living organisms. These relationships can be quite complex and play a major role for the survival or reproduction of species. Symbiosis can be positive, negative or neutral in nature for a species and may or may not be reciprocal. For this, there is a distinction between mutualism, commensalism, parasitism and the somewhat lesser known amensalism.

- **Mutualism** means both species benefit (for instance, flowers and insects: the flower benefits from the spreading of pollen and pollination, the insect benefits from the nectar provided as food).
- **Commensalism** means that only one of the two species benefits, but the other does not suffer any disadvantage. The benefiting species is the commensal (for instance, birds nesting in a tree, where the tree suffers no damage but also doesn't benefit: the bird is the commensal).
- **Parasitism** means only one party benefits (the parasite) at the expense of the other party who suffers (the host).
- **Amensalism** means no species benefits, but one of the species does experience a disadvantage (for instance, a tree providing shade that causes plants in the undergrowth to grow poorly: the tree has no advantage or disadvantage, but the undergrowth is affected).

predation The process in which a predator catches and eats a prey animal. It is an important interaction within an ecosystem. Species can undergo adaptations through selection for this reason: for example, the predator for a better hunting technique—and the prey for a better camouflage technique.

domesticated Plants or animals that humans have controlled in such a way that they are adapted to human desires, usually for utility. Animals are selected for desired behaviour (pets) or for efficient production (farm animals), plants for application (as raw material for fibres, or colour for aesthetics, for example) or for food production (such as protein richness or adaptations against diseases). Species thereby lose natural behaviour or other characteristics and often become dependent on humans.

---

native species Species naturally occurring in an area. Often an (arbitrary) year is chosen, such as before 1800. Newcomers (neophytes) may also fall into this category, provided they have arrived naturally. Native is sometimes confused with autochthonous, but autochthonous is really site-specific and means that a species has established itself geographically once since the ice ages. Autochthonous material of plants therefore means that it comes from the region and is genetically similar. Native only refers to the species itself, but not necessarily to its regional occurrence.

---

invasive species Species of animals or plants that should not naturally occur in an area, but have been introduced by humans, intentionally or unintentionally. These are also called exotic species. Invasive means that a species spreads widely, with negative consequences for native species. Invasive exotic species are often controlled to contain their spreading.

---

neophyte A newcomer. It is the term for plants that have established themselves in a place where they are not originally from, but are considered to have become native.

---

wild garden / ecological garden / biodiverse garden / nature garden Garden where the natural process has a proper role and biodiversity is the main goal. In an ecological garden, not everything (and in extremo: almost nothing) is planned, but the conditions are created as a starting point for what will naturally occur and develop. The maintenance of such a garden is tailor-made and serves the plants and animals that inhabit it. The maintenance is always extensive.

---

native garden - botanical garden Only native species are planted in a native garden (Dutch: heemtuin), species that originally belong to the local environment. The aim is to preserve and display (including for educational purposes) these species. Often, plant families are shown in their context by soil type. This type of garden can also be used for scientific research. A botanical garden is mainly a collection (scientific or otherwise) of native and exotic plants and is often also used to conserve and cultivate endangered species, allowing researchers to study species as well.

---

bird breeding season The period when birds start to build nests, up to and including the time when the young are fledged and leave the nest. It is not a period that can be summed up with a start and end date: many species have their own start time for this, and not every species has to incubate the eggs for the same length of time. Species may also have a second brood (or even more often). In addition, due to fluctuations in climate, when animals start and stop breeding may vary from year to year. Therefore, behaviour is leading and not the date: the breeding season should therefore always be determined according to the behaviour of the species.

---

extensive green roof An extensive green roof involves limited maintenance, less complex vegetation and a relatively thin substrate package. This includes sedum roofs.

---

intensive green roof An intensive green roof needs more complex vegetation, a thicker substrate layer and specific maintenance. This includes biodiversity roofs.

---

substrate Material on which a plant grows. This can be soil, but can also be a lime-rich mortar in a wall or an artificial roofing material on a green roof.

---

mating roost bats Site where bats mate, usually in autumn. A mating roost is often strategically located on the route between summer roost and winter roost, allowing males to attract females. The same sites are used year after year, although there is probably also a network of mating roosts per individual.

---

maternity roost bats The space where groups of female bats give birth to pups. Incidentally, this roost can also be inhabited by females that are not yet or no longer sexually mature. Maternity roosts are used for several months and then abandoned. Maternity roosts may consist of a few dozen animals up to hundreds together. A maternity roost is usually a different place from a mating, summer or winter roost.

---

winter roost/ mass winter roost bats The place with stable temperature and humidity. It can be used by solitary animals or small groups. But it can also involve hundreds to thousands of bats at a time, and is then referred to as a mass winter roost. These roosts can be located in caves or bunkers, but they are also known to be found in high-rise apartment buildings because these have a high heat buffering capacity and, with the right construction method, can provide a stable climate.

---

summer roost bats Locations where bats live, not being a maternity roost. These may be solitary animals or small groups (often of males, as many females are in maternity groups).

Anthropocene An unofficial but now widely used term for the geological epoch in which there is a demonstrable human influence on the Earth's geochemical and biological system. Officially, we are still living in the Holocene, but because the influence of humans is so great that it is changing the earth (think ecosystem change, climate change, greenhouse gases, biodiversity loss), the term is used to raise awareness of our tremendous (negative) impact in the geologically short time that humans have been around. The beginning of the Anthropocene is debated. But quite commonly, the year 2000 is used.

Symbiocene A self-coined term by environmental philosopher Glenn Albrecht, for a new era that awaits us. It is an era in which humans, nature and technology live together in balance and benefit from each other's existence.

---

anthropogenic Something that has come about as a result of human influence. Anthropogenic climate change, for example, is that change to the climate attributable to human causes such as the burning of fossil fuels and the resulting increase in greenhouse gases.

Red List A method used worldwide to assess the endangerment status of various plant and animal species based on trends. The purpose of the Red List is to draw attention to species threatened with extinction, that are vulnerable or face other serious threats, with the ultimate aim of promoting conservation measures.

SOME ARCHITECTURAL TERMS USED IN THIS BOOK
(explained for ecologists)

---

loggia A balcony within the body of a building: an outdoor space closed on three sides and located within the facade plane. The opening is in the facade. Usually, the loggia is located on the first floor.

cantilevered, projection A building element or structural component that is mounted on or wedged into the building wall on only one or two sides, and from there protrudes freely (without additional support outside the facade). For example, a balcony can be cantilevered, but so can an upper floor of a tall building.

---

cavity, cavity wall and cavity leaf A wall construction consisting of an inner wall and an outer wall—also called inner and outer leaf—with an air space (the cavity) between them. Traditionally, the walls were made of masonry, but nowadays they also consist of other materials that protect the air cavity from weather conditions. A cavity contributes to the thermal insulation of the building, but for today's energy requirements, air alone is not enough. Therefore, an extra layer of insulation is added in the cavity (but there still remains a, narrower, ventilated air cavity on the outer side). For cavity walls that are not additionally insulated in this way (houses built before around 1980), the cavity is often subsequently filled with insulating foam or pellets, preventing animals from taking up residence there.

PROJECTS LIST

The House of Music, Budapest, Sou Fujimoto, 2022, HU / p. 5

La cité des Étoiles, Givors, Jean Renaudie, 1974/1981, FR / p. 12, 21

Ecokathedraal, Mildam, Louis G. le Roy, from ca. 1970 continual, NL / p. 18

Waldspirale, Darmstadt, Friedensreich Hundertwasser, Heinz M. Springmann, 1998 – 2000, D / p. 18

Foot bridge, Wald-Ruhestettenjk, Baubotanik, 2005, D / p. 22

Urban Reef, Urban Reef, 2023, NL / p. 23

Folly BAT, Studio Architectuur MAKEN, 2023, NL / p. 25

Öko-Häuser, Berlin Frei Otto, 1989-1991, D / p. 39

Baumhaus, Darmstadt, Ot Hoffmann, 1968-1972, D / p. 40, 44-45

Vertical, Amsterdam, DS landscape architects, 2016, NL / p. 56

De Warren, Amsterdam, Natrufied, 2023, NL / p. 61

Groene Mient, The Hague, Francois Verhoeven, Dennis Fillié and Dennis Hofman, 2020, NL / p. 62

Tuinstraat, Lange Riddersstraat, Municipality of Antwerp, 2021, B / p. 62

Grasdachsiedlung Laher Wiese, Hannover, Boockhoff & Rentrop, 1984/1987, D / p. 63

Bosco Verticale, Milan, Stefano Boeri Architetti, 2014, IT / p. 67, 178

The Standard Hotel, High Line, New York, Ennead, 2009, US / p. 67

Residential building Groenmarkt, Amsterdam, Ronald Janssen architects, Bastiaan Jongerius architects, Buro Harro, 2022, NL / p. 67, 169

Woning Axel Ghyssaert, Brughes, A. Ghyssaert, 1969, B / p. 67

Biesbosch Museumeiland, Werkendam, Studio Marco Vermeulen, 2015, NL / p. 67

Residential building Groenmarkt Medina, Eindhoven, Neave Brown, 2003, NL / p. 67

Woon- en werkgebouw Het Platform, Utrecht, VenhoevenCS, 2020, NL / p. 67

The Valley, Amsterdam, MVRDV, 2022, NL / p. 67

Stadskantoor Venlo, Kraaijvanger Architects, 2016, NL / p. 68-69

Maggie's Yorkshire, Leeds, Heatherwick Studio, Balston Agius, 2012, GB / p. 70-71

École des sciences et de la biodiversité, Boulogne-Billancourt, Paris, ChartierDalix, 2014, FR / p. 72-77, 178

Parkeergarage, Delft, wUrck architecture urban design landscape, 2022, NL / p. 78-79

Trekvlietzone, The Hague, Flux Landscape Architecture, 2018, NL / p. 88

Stadthaus M1, Freiburg, Barkow+Leibinger, 2013, D / p. 92, 188-189

Groendak parkeergarage, European Patent Office, Rijswijk, Copijn, 1997, NL / p. 96, 97

Zorgwoningen De Eiken, Zoersel, Monnikenheide, UR architects, 2020, B / p. 98

Vegetated sitting stairs, campus TU Delft, Delft, René Hoonhout, CRE, 2018, NL / p. 102

Biotope City, Wienerberg, IBA, Vienna, various architects, 2013-2021, AT / p. 104-105

Het Zandkasteel, Amsterdam, Architectenbureau Alberts & Van Huut / Garden- and landschapsarchitects Jørn & Lia Copijn, 1986, transformation: Timo Cents & Arcadis, 2023, NL / p. 106-107

The Barbican, London, Nigel Dunnett, 2015, GB / p. 108-109

Vanishing Staircase, Utrecht, Birthe Leemeijer, Vergroening Singel030, 2018, NL / p. 110-111

Ecolumn, Faunus Nature Creations, 2022, NL / p. 122-123

Bat Tower, Buffalo, NY, Joyce Hwang, 2021, US / p. 122-123

Faunamuur, Almere, Utopia Eiland, 2020, NL / p. 122-123

Gierzwaluwtoren, Warsaw, Menthol architects, 2013, PL / p. 122-123

Aeres Hogeschool, Almere, BDG Architects, 2021, NL / p. 124-125

De Rots, Vertical, Amsterdam, Studio Donna van Milligen Bielke, 2023, NL / p. 130

Beestenboom, Gemeente Westland, Finbarr McComb Architect, LOLA Landscape Architects and Aqua Terra Nova, 2016, NL / p. 133

Bridge for Laboratory Sciences, Vassar College, Poughkeepsie, Ennead Architects, 2016, US / p. 134

Triodosbank, Driebergen, RAU Architects, Arcadis, 2019, NL / p. 142-143

Pound bat towers, Ransdorp, Nieuwendam, Amsterdam, Ruimtelab, Batweter, 2021, NL / p. 148

Kattenbrug, Groningen, Korth Tielens architecten, DS landscapsarchitects, 2023, NL / p. 153

L'Oasis d'Aboukir, Paris, Patrick Blanc, 2013, FR / p. 164

Woongebouw Het Funen, Amsterdam, Geurst & Schulze, 2007, NL / p. 167, 184

Hoofdkantoor AP-HP hôpitaux, Paris, ChartierDalix, 2022, FR / p. 167, 180

Ricola Europe, Mulhouse, Herzog&deMeuron, 1993, CH / p. 167

Edison Lite, Paris, Manuelle Gautrand Architecture, Bureau Bas Smets, 2020, FR / p. 168

Hortus Ludi, Nijmegen, Studio Architectuur MAKEN, 2023, NL / p. 170

Minervahaven, Amsterdam, De Dakdokters, 2022, NL / p. 173

Natuurlijk wonen, Westbroek, ORGA architect, 2022, NL / p. 174

Bicycle storage, IJboulevard Amsterdam, VenhoevenCS, DS landschapsarchitecten, 2023, NL / p. 176

Green bus shelters, Utrecht, Gemeente Utrecht, 2021, NL / p. 177

National Museum Oslo, Kleihues + Schuwerk, 2021, N / p. 180

Genderdal, Eindhoven, Buro Lubbers, 2013, NL / p. 180

MTV building, London, Biotecture, 2015, GB / p. 180

Building that grows, Montpellier, Maison Edouard François, 2000, FR / p. 180

Technical space, Malmö, Galeasens Gränd, SE / p. 180

Lumengebouw, Wageningen, Behnisch Architekten, 1998, NL / p. 183

Busstation, Heerlen, Michel Huisman, 2008, NL / p. 183

Student housing, Munich, Fink+Jocher, 2005, D / p. 183

MFO-Park, Zürich, Burckhardt, 2002, CH / p. 183

House N, Tokyo, Sou Fujimoto, 2008, JP / p. 183

Biodiversity wall, Rue Buffon, ChartierDalix, 2021, FR / p. 186

Bioreceptive concrete, Respyre, NL / p. 187

M6B2 Tower of Biodiversity, Paris, Maison Édouard François, 2016, FR / p. 190-193

25 Verde, Turin, Luciano Pia, 2012, IT / p. 194-195

SUND Nature Park, Copenhagen, SLA Landscape architects, C.F. Møller Architects, 2018, DK / p. 196-197

Amstelstroombrug, Amsterdam, VenhoevenCS architecure+urbanism, Smartland landscape architecture, 2022, NL / p. 198/199

Green Quay walls, Amsterdam, Municipality of Amsterdam, NL / p. 200-201

De Utrechtse Steen, Amersfoort, Ruimtelab, NL / p. 201

Wall Garden, Delft, NL / p. 201

Green Quays, Breda, NL / p. 201

Torre Guinigi, Lucca, 13e eeuw, IT / p. 213

Credits

AUTHORS:: Jacques Vink, Piet Vollaard, Niels de Zwarte
COPY-EDITING: Leo Reijnen, Taal & Teken / **TRANSLATION:** Jean Tee
PHOTO EDITING: Jacques Vink, Niels de Zwarte, Yvo Zijlstra, Sara Duisters
DESIGN & LITHOGRAPHY: Yvo Zijlstra (Antenna-men) / **ILLUSTRATIONS:** Jane Bergkotte
PRINTING: Wilco Art Books / **PAPER:** 120 grs Maxi Offset
PRODUCTION: Marja Jager, nai010 publishers
PUBLISHER: Marcel Witvoet, nai010 publishers

THIS PUBLICATION WAS MADE POSSIBLE, IN PART, BY: Creative Industries Fund NL, BPD Cultuurfonds, Bureau Stadsnatuur, City of Rotterdam, J.E. Jurriaanse Stichting, Ministry of Agriculture, Nature and Food Quality

FRONT COVER: Little owl by Robert Harding/ INSIDE FRONTCOVER: A protist being surrounded by a healthy network of decomposer fungi / IMAGE RIGHT: 'London starling gang' by Tomos Brangwyn / IMAGE SPREADS: P3: Magpie uses anti-bird pins to build its nest / P5: In Great Britain some 650 species of beetles are associated with dead wood / P26: Common whitlowgrass / P46: Bacteria and mold growing on agar plates from soil samples / P80: Starlings / P126: Urban Gardening at Tempelhofer Feld (Flughafen Tempelhof) in Berlin, D / P144: Close up of coral fungi on the woodland floor in autumn / P160: Greylag geese / P214: An urban fox / P222: Grey-backed mining bee.

IMAGE CREDITS: P2: Auke-Florian Hiemstra / P4: György Palkó / P8: collage Ross Piper (images courtesy of Udo Schmidt and Lech Borowiec) / P14, 15: CC / P15: Flickr, Mike McBey CC / P18: Peter Wouda / P19, 38, 39, 86, 106, 118, 183, 213: Wikimedia CC, Von Ludvig / P20: Mike Davies / P22: Office for Living Architecture / P23: Urban Reef / P24: Aaron Escobar / P25, 170: Studio Architectuur MAKEN / P26: Sanne Luijben / P30: Zack Aboulazm / P33: CC World of data: Hannah Ritchie / P34: Alexandra Arènes / P36: Remko Andeweg / P40: Ot Hoffmann / P41, 86, 96, 97, 119, 149, 158, 202, 204: Niels de Zwarte / P41: Ed Hawkins / P41: Karin van der Wiel, KNMI / P42, 43: Azote for Stockholm Resilience Centre, based on analysis in Richardson et al 2023 / P44: Dirk Junklewitz / P46: Shutterstock / P126, 144, 160, 214: Alamy / P56, 176 : DS landschapsarchitecten / P61 – CPO De Warren / P62: François Venhoeven / P62: Jeroen Broeckx / P64: Menno Reemer / P64, 118, 119, 222: Mark Grutters / P67: Dimitar Harizano / P67, 169: Jeroen Musch / P67: Bruno Vanbesien / P67, 68, 68: Ronald Tilleman / P67, 142: Ossip van Duivenbode / P68 Kraaijvanger / P68 Stijn Poelstra / P71: ©Hufton+Crow / P72: P. Guignard / P75: ©ChartierDalix, photography by Myr Muratet / P76, 77: ©ChartierDalix, photography by Takuji Shimmura / P76, 178: ©ChartierDalix / P78: Stephan Nierop/ P80: Adobe stock / P84: Jeffrey Milstein / P86: Susanne Kuijpers / P87, 136, 139, 149: Garry Bakker / P88: Flux Landscape Architecture / P88: Marco Tanis / P88 – pxbay / P92, 157, 188: Stefan Müller / P95: Willem Braam / P95: Mark Grutters / P98: Michiel De Cleene / P98: UR Architects / P100, 102, 102, 102, 133, 133, 176, 180, 184, 200: Jacques Vink / P104: Helga Fassbinder / P106: Timo Cents / P108: Nigel Dunnett / P110: Lies König / P112 – CC Wikimedia, Shawn Caza / P117 – Buginn / P118, 156: Cora de Groot / P119: Menno Reemer / P121: pixbay / P121: Josephine Beijer / P121: Wouter Moerland / P122: Ecolumn / P122: Joyce Hwang / P125: Gerard van Beek / P128: Mark van Soest / P130: Studio Donna van Milligen Bielke / P33: Danny Taheij / P134: Richard Barnes / P137: Jasper Doest / P138: Monica van Kleef / P139: Rinus Heykoop/ P142: Bert Rietberg / P146: Johann Prescher / P148: Roos Aldershoff / P149: René Janssen / P151: Unitura / P153: Dennis De Smet / P158: Joek Roex / P158 – CC Wikimedia, James Gathany / P158: Pepijn van der Spek / P167, 180: Camille Gharbi / P167: Herzog&deMeuron / P168: Luc Boegly / P169: Harro de Jong / P170: Maarten van Apeldoorn / P173, 174: De Dakdokters / P174: Wij-Zien.nl / P176: VenhoevenCS architecture+urbanism / P178: Laura Cionci / P178: City of Utrecht, Barbra Verbij / P180: Alwin de Lang / P180: Biotecture / P180: Maison Edouard Francois / P183: Frank Ockert / P183: Benjamin Hosking / P183: Burckhardt Architektur / P183: Fink+Jocher / P186: Olivier Genevoix / P187: Ronan Kok / P188: Ina Reinecke / P188: Annemiek Bongers / P191, 192: Pierre L'Excellent / P194, 195: Beppe Giardino / P196: Jakob Damkjær / P196: Jens Lindhe / P199: Luuk Kramer Photography, Amsterdam / P199: Paul Poels video- en fotografie / P200: Ton Denters, City of Amsterdam / P205: Judith Tielemans / P213: Wikimedia CC.

nai010 publishers is an internationally orientated publisher specialized in developing, producing and distributing books in the fields of architecture, urbanism, art and design. www.nai010.com

nai010 books are available internationally at selected bookstores and from the following distribution partners: North, Central and South America - Artbook | D.A.P., New York, USA, dap@dapinc.com / Rest of the world - Idea Books, Amsterdam, the Netherlands, idea@ideabooks.nl / For general questions, please contact nai010 publishers directly at sales@nai010.com or visit our website www.nai010.com for further information.

Printed and bound in the Netherlands

ISBN 978-94-6208-811-5

Building Urban Nature. Towards a Nature-Inclusive Architecture is also available in Dutch (*Stadsnatuur bouwen. Naar een natuurinclusieve architectuur*) and as e-book: ISBN 978-94-6208-821-4 (e-book)

Het Natuurhistorisch
Bureau Stadsnatuur
Ministry of Agriculture, Nature and Food Quality
City of Rotterdam
bpd cultuurfonds
J.E. Jurriaanse Stichting
creative industries fund NL